INSTANT
HAUTE
CUISINE

French Cooking — American Style

Also by Esther Riva Solomon

INSTANT ITALIAN CUISINE

INSTANT HAUTE CUISINE

French Cooking—American Style

by

Esther Riva Solomon

M. EVANS & COMPANY, INC.
New York

M. Evans and Company titles are distributed in
the United States by the J. B. Lippincott Company,
East Washington Square, Philadelphia, Pa. 19105;
and in Canada by McClelland & Stewart Ltd.,
25 Hollinger Road, Toronto M4B 3G2, Ontario

Designed by James Darby

Library of Congress Catalog Card Number: 63-9771

ISBN 0-87131-247-6 (paperback)
ISBN 0-87131-063-5 (casebound)

Manufactured in the United States of America

9 8 7 6 5 4 3 2 1

To Irwin, the home where my heart is.

Preface

Like so many other non-professional cooks, I learned and developed my culinary skill in many ways. The basic rudiments of the art came from my mother. Then, learning by doing, by experimentation, from cookbooks and gifted friends, I eventually reached a point at which I could consider myself a good cook and a successful hostess.

Reading French recipes and French cookbooks of classic cuisine had become a small passion of mine. Leafing through their pages, mentally tasting the subtle and exotic flavors of *haute cuisine*, I thought . . . if only I could cook like that. No wonder, when the opportunity of going to Paris to study at the celebrated Cordon Bleu presented itself, I snapped at it.

Cordon Bleu was everything I'd hoped it would be, but the most valuable thing I learned there was a principle that would have surprised the chef. To him it was impossible to turn out *haute cuisine* — classic French cookery — without spending hours in the kitchen, going through countless steps of preparation. Most American women don't have that kind of time. Fortunately almost anyone can copy French masterpieces quickly, and so well that most people can't tell the difference. I call the technique Instant Haute Cuisine.

The chef looked just the way I hoped a real French chef would look. M. Charles Narses was fat and rosy and full of good spirits. He did everything with dash and precision. Chopping an onion with a blur of his big knife, he would look at us slyly, as if to say, "Wasn't that marvelous?" And we students, seated on a bank of wooden platforms, would murmur appreciatively.

The chef had two kitchen boys, bright youngsters of fourteen or fifteen and excellent cooks themselves. He kept them hopping. At his gesture the right pot would appear in his hand. The boys had obviously done a lot of the work before class — cleaned the vegetables, cut up the chicken, and attended to other chores we couldn't even guess at. The chef often stopped to teach them things he thought they, as his appentices, should know.

The kitchen at Cordon Bleu was a surprise. I'd expected a room with walls of stone and a beamed ceiling, gleaming rows of copper pots and a big black stove with a caldron of stock simmering away. Instead, the kitchen was an immaculate white with an unspectacular sink and an ordinary electric range. All the pots and pans were of heavy aluminum. There was a chopping block and three small waist-high ovens, which the chef controlled partly with a thermostat and partly by sticking his hand inside to see if the temperature felt right. There were no mixers, blenders, beaters, choppers, or similar devices, which I consider indispensable.

I'd expected the chef to begin with "how to prepare stock," or "basic dishes" or "first we'll take the sauces." Instead, he started demonstrating one major dish after another. I felt sure I'd be lost, but general principles soon began to emerge — the importance of measuring exactly, for example. The chef said that the test of a really good cook is to make a dish the same way every time. To do that, your preparation must be the same. It was amazing to see how carefully the chef prepared a *pilaf*, the foundation of many of the dishes he made. If the first time he took a spoonful of rice and a spoonful of broth, the second time he took a spoonful of rice and a spoonful of broth, and again the third time. Timing, too, must be precise. His *pilaf* took twenty-three minutes in a 325° oven, and that was it. He was a perfectionist — a man whose skills I could never hope to equal, only to imitate.

I picked up many helpful techniques at Cordon Bleu. The dishes themselves were splendid, but deep inside of me panic was building. How in the world could I devote four or five hours to a single dish? That's what it might take an amateur cook like me, starting from scratch and without a kitchen boy. If that was what good French cooking required, it could never transform our daily dining. I remember how frustrated I felt one day when the chef was doing *poulet à l'estragon*, chicken breasts in a creamy, tarragon-flavored sauce. It took that skillful man one hour and a dozen pots to make his chicken gravy. I was awed even before I tasted it. And it *was* good. But as I sampled it, I realized with a jolt that it tasted just like a good canned gravy I'd bought from time to time back home. *It's just one ingredient in a complex recipe*, I thought, *I could use that canned gravy and no one would ever know.*

I tried to dismiss the wild notion; it seemed to contradict the whole idea of coming to Cordon Bleu. But as soon as I got back to the United States, I tried *poulet à l'estragon* with the canned gravy and two other short cuts — prepared foods I knew were every bit as good as anything I could make. It worked beautifully.

Those three canned ingredients in my *poulet à l'estragon* represent the first rule of Instant Haute Cuisine — *substitute*. At Cordon Bleu, most of the recipes involved several mixing bowls, a couple of pots, six things to clean up, and many, many steps. I began to see that the more involved the dish, the less each subtlety matters in the total taste picture. The more steps, the more you can substitute and get the same effect. For example, if you are making a broth that you are going to serve as a broth, you must start with chicken, bones, and so on, and make it. But if, as for *poulet à l'estragon*, you need a broth simply to stew chicken in, a can of good chicken broth will do nicely.

While the other students at Cordon Bleu took copious notes, I found myself watching for ingredients which I could duplicate with the best of the processed foods available in supermarkets back home. Potato soup, for example. So many French soups start with potatoes. But there's at least one excellent frozen potato soup I can buy almost anywhere. By substituting it in my *potage grand duc* recipe (cream of cauliflower soup), I can save more than an hour of work. The soup manufacturer has already done the work for me.

Take advantage of processed foods of good quality. By "good quality" I don't necessarily mean "expensive"; I mean foods that are just right for the purpose. Ideas still occur to me as I look over the frozen-food cases and canned-goods shelves of the local food markets. New products are constantly showing up. Watching for them and trying them in a recipe can pay off in time saved.

The boned and skinned chicken breasts required for the *poulet à l'estragon* call into play the second rule of Instant Haute Cuisine — *cut down on time-consuming hand labor*. In this case, use the expert services offered by neighborhood butchers, and the men behind the scenes at supermarket meat counters. Once upon a time I'd tried to debone a chicken myself and found it very hard work. And so when I was shopping for my "instant" *poulet à l'estragon*,

I mustered my courage and rang that little bell marked SERVICE. "Here are four chicken breasts," I said to the man who appeared at the window. "Please bone them and remove the skin." There was a small charge for the service, but the butcher, an expert, saved me literally hours of time and effort.

There are certain ingredients which the chef at Cordon Bleu used over and over again, recipe after recipe. Each time he would stop and prepare them — green butter for instance, a blend of butter, lemon juice, chives, and parsley, which may be spooned over a steak, green beans, or artichoke hearts. No American housewife, I said to myself, would duplicate effort like that. We were trained to be more efficient.

That brought me to the third rule for cooking French-style while keeping your sanity — *mass produce*. If there is something I'm going to use five times a week, I make it once and have it on hand. Green butters refrigerate nicely. So does *beurre manié*, the little balls of butter and flour which are used for last-minute thickening of gravies. And in the freezer I keep such commercially mass-produced necessities as frozen chopped chives, parsley, chopped onion, small peeled white potatoes, and tiny carrots.

The rule of mass production leads naturally into the fourth rule — *work ahead*. At Cordon Bleu I wasn't the only student to complain, "This takes so long! I'd never get finished!" The chef would reply, "Now really, you can make this the day before and it will do perfectly well." A surprisingly large number of goods keep well. Meringues stay fresh for days. An un-iced cake, wrapped in foil, is just as good several days after baking. Hollandaise sauce can be prepared the day before and reheated at the last minute. Prepare the meat or fish and the sauce ahead, the chef advised, but don't combine them until the last minute.

A number of my friends have tried Instant Haute Cuisine and are sold on it. Together we've developed the fifth rule — *copy only the best*. If the recipe is complicated but not very distinguished to begin with, there is no point in going to the trouble of simplifying it.

Turning out meals for guests who expected something spectacularly French, I discovered my sixth and last rule — *don't skimp on the decoration*. French food must look French. If I put a gob of chocolate pudding in a glass dish, it's chocolate pudding. If I put it in a French-looking tiny white porcelain pot, it becomes *petit pot de crème au chocolat*. Put a crystallized violet (you buy them at candy stores) on top of vanilla ice cream — suddenly it's French.

A word of warning, though. There are pitfalls for the hostess who earns a reputation for serving elegant French cuisine. You can't keep turning out special food day after day, even for guests. One Saturday evening I decided to take a night off. Our guest was a close friend. She's a gentle, soft-spoken woman, but when I put the entrée on the table, disappointment got the better of her. "What!" she said. "You have me for dinner and serve just steak?"

How This Book Came To Be Written

The short-cuts and substitutions that make up the recipes for Instant Haute Cuisine worked so well for me that I got to thinking that others might like to learn about these methods.

The food editor at *The Saturday Evening Post* agreed, and as a result *French Food — U.S. Style*, an article which outlined the techniques with a number of exemplary recipes, was published last May. I had always known that the *Post* had a mammoth circulation — but I had never dreamed that so many of its readers were women interested in the fine art of *haute cuisine*. The response was staggering. The people at the *Post* told me that they only forwarded on to me a part of the mail they received — those letters which asked special questions. All I know is that it took me two solid weeks to answer all my mail. Enough of the letters asked for more recipes and more detail on technique that I was encouraged to expand my *Post* story into a book. Unlike most books, this one was written on request. I hope the ideas in it will work for you as well as they have for me.

E.R.S.

Contents

APPETIZERS

HORS D'OEUVRES
QUICHE LORRAINE
PATE MAISON
RADIS AU BEURRE
OEUFS EN GELEE
CAVIAR BLINI
CAVIAR FRAIS
CAVIAR PERSIMMON
CAVIAR ENDIVE
PATE EN GELEE
ESCARGOTS FROIDS
CRABES AU RIZ
HUITRES MOSCOU
MOULES MAYONNAISES
SAUMON FUME
CORNETS DE JAMBON
HOMARD EN CROUTE
TOMATES AUX CREVETTES
SAUCISSONS
COEUR A LA CREME
ASPERGES FRANCAISES
ARTICHAUTS FROIDS
CROQUE MADAME
FONDUE SUISSE
CELERI REMOULADE

Appetizers
Without
Toothpicks

A 'little something first' can be something hot, or something cold, something that just whets the appetite, or something that would serve as a main course if the portions were bigger. It can be vegetable or fish, pickled or plain, on toast, or on a plate. But whatever it is, it can *not* be served on a toothpick or dipped with a potato chip. Not if you want to eat French style.

Anchovies, Pimiento, and Artichoke Hearts

You'll Need:

1 can flat anchovies   1 small can artichoke hearts
              1 can whole pimientos

How To:

Drain pimientos and place on plate. Lay 2 anchovies on top and 2 more crosswise on the first ones. Surround with artichoke hearts. Repeat 3 times. Pass oil, red wine vinegar, and a pepper grinder. *Serves: 4*

Red Kidney Bean Salad, Tuna Fish, and Scallions

You'll Need:

1 (1-pound) can red kidney   1 (7-ounce) can tuna fish
  beans, drained   4 scallions
½ cup bottled Italian salad   4 lemon wedges
  dressing

How To:

Mix kidney beans with Italian dressing. Refrigerate. Make 4 individual servings. Pile kidney beans on plate. Put chunk of tuna next to it, lemon wedge on top. One scallion on each plate. *Serves: 4*

19

Ceci Pea Salad, Salami and Pimiento

You'll Need:

1 (No. 1 tall) can ceci
  (chick) peas, drained
½ cup bottled Italian salad
  dressing
1 tablespoon chopped chives
  or parsley

8 thin slices Genoa salami,
  cut from the roll on a slant
  so they are oval
1 can whole pimientos

How To:

Combine ceci peas, dressing, and chives. Put in center of plate. Surround with slices of salami and pimiento. *Serves: 4*

QUICHE LORRAINE

Egg Custard, Ham and Cheese Tart

You'll Need:

1 9-inch pie crust, partly
  baked (made from a
  ready-mix according
  to directions on package)
¼ pound sliced boiled ham
4 eggs

2 egg yolks
½ cup light cream
4 tablespoons grated
  Parmesan cheese
½ teaspoon salt
A grind of black pepper

How To:

Mix pastry as described on package, line pie dish, bake in 475° oven only 5 minutes. Let cool. Cut the ham into shreds. Use scissors, if you like. Put in bottom of pie crust. Combine rest of ingredients in a bowl. Beat with a wire whisk until they are well mixed. Pour into the pie crust. Bake in a 300° oven for 40 minutes. Check for doneness. If custard

is set, Quiche is done. Cut like a pie and serve at once.
Serves: 6

Extra Touches: Substitute ½ pound of sliced bacon for the ham. Cook bacon and crumble. Put in bottom of pie. Add 2 tablespoons of bacon fat to the custard mixture. It is nice to serve the Quiche from the same dish that you bake it in. Any shallow casserole will do, oval or round.

PATE MAISON

Pâté Maison

You'll Need:

1 small can French truffles	1 envelope (1 tablespoon)
2 ounces (¼ cup) brandy	unflavored gelatin
¾ cup canned chicken broth	1 pound liverwurst

How To:

Open truffles the night before. Chop one truffle, slice the other. Soak all truffles in the brandy. Next morning put broth in pan, add gelatin, heat only until gelatin is dissolved. Put liverwurst in large bowl, break up with a fork. Add hot broth, chopped truffle, and brandy. Beat with electric mixer. Put in refrigerator to chill. When firm, beat again. This time place in oiled mold. When firm, unmold and decorate with brandied slices of black truffle. *Serves: 18*

Extra Touches: If you are all out of truffles, and this does happen, substitute 2 tablespoons of blanched slivered almonds (they come in cans) and a dozen black olives, sliced or chopped.

RADIS AU BEURRE

Radishes with Butter

You'll Need:

Bunch of fresh radishes
Salt

½ pound sweet whipped
butter

How To:

Leave some of the green leaves on the radishes. Pile radishes on individual plates with a lump of sweet butter. Serve with a small knife, so that each person can butter his radish, take a bite, put some more butter on it, and so on. Pass the salt.
Serves: 6

Extra Touches: There is a special kitchen device that slices radishes in a spiral so that the radish pulls apart like an accordion. Slice the radishes in this fashion. Pull apart. Spread with softened butter and snap back into its original shape. It saves your guests buttering their own radishes.
Good as an accompaniment to toast spread with anchovy butter. Delicious next to a slice of pâté.

OEUFS EN GELEE

Eggs in Aspic

You'll Need:

6 eggs
1 (10½-ounce) can beef
    bouillon
    Watercress or lettuce

1 envelope (1 tablespoon)
    gelatin
6 molds, such as custard cups,
    egg cups, or a 6-cup muffin
    tin

How To:

Cover eggs with cold water, bring to boiling, and boil about 4 minutes. Or lower eggs gently into boiling water and simmer about 8 minutes. Remove from heat and run under cold water. Let stand until eggs are cold. Peel and place one egg in each mold. Dissolve gelatin in bouillon (heated) and, when cool, pour over eggs. Place in refrigerator to set. To serve: unmold each onto a bed of watercress or lettuce leaves. Serve with mayonnaise. *Serves: 6*

Extra Touches: Put a small slice of ham in each mold in addition to the egg. The egg is not supposed to be hardcooked. Don't feel you've made a mistake when you find the yellow is runny. This dish is also good made with poached eggs.

CAVIAR BLINI

Caviar Rolled in Thin Pancakes

You'll Need:

1 dozen thin buckwheat
    pancakes (hot)
4 tablespoons melted butter
    (hot)

½ pint sour cream (cold)
4 tablespoons red or pressed
    black caviar

How To:

Make buckwheat pancakes using a mix, and follow directions on package. Pour a little melted butter over each cake as it is taken from the griddle. Put a tablespoon of sour cream in the center of each pancake, then a teaspoon of red or black caviar on the sour cream. Fold pancakes over caviar and sour cream. Serve 2 pancakes to each person. *Serves: 6*

CAVIAR FRAIS

Fresh Caviar

If some rich uncle dies and leaves you a stock of fresh caviar, just put it in a chilled silver bowl on ice, with a silver spoon, and let everybody help themselves. Don't worry about details, but crackers or thin toast should be on hand. If no silver bowl, use your best crystal or glass. The classic way to serve fresh caviar is on thin toast, sprinkled with finely chopped hard-cooked egg and minced onion.

CAVIAR PERSIMMON

Persimmon Quarter with Caviar

You'll Need:

1 teaspoon black caviar for each persimmon

1 persimmon for each person
1 slice fresh lime, each

How To:

Quarter the persimmon. Place a teaspoon of caviar in the center. Serve with a slice of lime.

CAVIAR ENDIVE

Belgian Endive Stuffed with Caviar

You'll Need:

Belgian endive

Red and pressed black caviar

How To:

Separate the leaves of a stalk of Belgian endive, wash, wrap in waxed paper and chill. Stuff the leaves as you would stuff celery. Use red caviar and black. Serve 4 stuffed leaves on a plate, 2 stuffed with red caviar, 2 stuffed with black.

PATE EN GELEE

Pâté in Ruby Jelly

You'll Need:

2 envelopes(or 2 tablespoons) unflavored gelatin
2 (12½-ounce) cans jellied madrilène
½ (10½-ounce) can light chicken broth

Red pure-food coloring
1 small can truffles (each can contains 2 or 3 truffles)
½ cup brandy
1 pound liverwurst

How To:

The day before, slice one truffle, chop the rest. Add truffles and juice to ½ cup brandy. Store in refrigerator. Dissolve 1 envelope (or tablespoon) of gelatin in 2 cans of madrilène. Add a few drops of red pure-food coloring. Pour some of this mixture into a 2-quart mold, just enough to line the bottom with ¼ inch of aspic. Place mold in refrigerator. When aspic thickens but is not completely firm, arrange 6 slices of truffle in it. Return to refrigerator to harden. Pour remaining aspic in a bowl in the refrigerator to become firm. Dissolve 1 envelope of gelatin in ¼ can of light chicken broth. Heat, and pour this mixture into a large mixing bowl. Add chopped truffles, truffle juice, brandy, and all the liverwurst. Beat with an electric beater or by hand until all ingredients are thoroughly mixed; it will look runny and wet. Put it into the refrigerator to set. When set, beat again. Pile this liver pâté into the mold that is already lined with ruby aspic. Chill until set. Turn out onto a chilled serving platter. Chop the extra aspic. Surround the molded liver pâté with this chopped aspic. Serve with toast. *Serves: 18*

ESCARGOTS FROIDS

Cold Snails in Mustard Mayonnaise

You'll Need:

1 can snails (containing 24
  snails)
¾ cup mayonnaise
1 teaspoon dry mustard

2 tablespoons chopped green
  herbs such as parsley
  and/or chives

How To:

Drain snails. Combine the rest of the ingredients to make a mayonnaise with a mustard flavor. Mix drained snails with half the mayonnaise. Arrange on lettuce leaves. Top with rest of mayonnaise. Serve very cold. *Serves: 4*

Extra Touches: Some canned snails have a plastic container of shells attached. If you get this kind, mix the snails with half the mayonnaise. Put each snail into a snail shell. This will fill most but not all of the shell. Fill the rest with mayonnaise. Chill thoroughly.

CRABES AU RIZ

Crab Meat with Rice

You'll Need:

1 cup rice
1 cup mayonnaise
1 tablespoon lemon juice
2 tablespoons capers

3 tablespoons chopped
  parsley
1-pound can of fresh crab
  meat, or 1 pound frozen
  crab meat

How To:

Cook the rice according to directions on the package. Mix a cup of mayonnaise with the lemon juice, half the capers, and half the parsley. Cool. Mix the cooked rice with half of the mayonnaise mixture. To serve, make a bed of rice on a chilled serving dish. Pile crab meat in the center. Cover crab meat with remaining mayonnaise. Sprinkle with the rest of the capers and chopped parsley. *Serves: 4*

Extra Touches: Use fresh or canned lobster meat, cooked cleaned shrimps, langoustines, or king crab fingers instead of crab meat.

HUITRES MOSCOU

Oysters with Caviar

You'll Need:

3 dozen oysters on half shell
   Shaved ice
1 lemon
   Coarse-ground pepper
12 ounces (tablespoons) black
   caviar

Thin-sliced brown bread (the square-cut sour pumpernickel type)
Sweet butter

How To:

Arrange drained oysters on the half shell on a bed of shaved ice, in soup plates. Squeeze a drop of lemon juice on each oyster. Add a dash of pepper. Put a spoon of caviar on each oyster. Serve with triangles of buttered brown bread. *Serves: 6*

Note: If you can't get oysters on the half shell, put your oysters on watercress on ice and go on from there.

MOULES MAYONNAISES

Cold Mussels with Mustard-Mayonnaise Sauce

You'll Need:

½ cup mayonnaise
½ cup sour cream
1 teaspoon dry mustard
3 tablespoons chopped green
  assorted herbs, parsley,
  chives, green onion, even

pickle qualifies as an herb
  this time
1 (1-pint) can mussels
  (drained)
1 tablespoon chopped parsley
Lettuce

How To:

Mix everything together except the mussels, parsley, and lettuce. This is the sauce. Combine mussels with half the sauce. Serve on lettuce leaves. Coat with remaining sauce. Sprinkle with chopped parsley. *Serves: 6*

Extra Touches: Surround with sliced pickled onion rings. You'll find them in jars of cocktail fixings.

SAUMON FUME

Smoked Salmon

You can buy smoked salmon at a delicatessen. There they slice as much as you want off the big fish. Nova Scotia smoked salmon has the most delicate flavor. The variety called *lox* is a bit salty. You can also buy both varieties of sliced smoked salmon in cans.

How To Serve:

Place a slice or two of smoked salmon on each plate. Sprinkle with drained capers, about 6 to a serving. Add a lemon wedge to each plate. Pass a pepper grinder. Serve with it thin-sliced dark pumpernickel bread and sweet butter.

CORNETS DE JAMBON

Stuffed Ham Cones

You'll Need:

1 cup cooked frozen mixed vegetables (½ a package of seasoned peas and celery, or corn and tomatoes, would do)
1 (10½-ounce) can beef consommé

½ envelope (or ½ tablespoon) unflavored gelatin
6 slices boiled ham
6 cone-shaped paper cups
1 extra paper cup*

How To:

Cook vegetables. Drain. Dissolve gelatin in consommé and mix with vegetables. Put in refrigerator and allow to thicken. Fit a slice of ham into each cup, lining it around the inside. Trim edges with scissors so that the ham fits exactly. Fill with the thickened gelatin mixture. Return cups to refrigerator to set firmly. Just before serving, unmold. *Serves: 6*

Extra Touches: You have 6 cornets of ham. Arrange them on a circular platter with the points in toward the center like a wheel.

* Fill extra paper cup with mayonnaise. Cut off the point. When you squeeze the paper cup, the mayonnaise will run out of the hole in a thin stream. Use this to decorate the cornets as you like.

HOMARD EN CROUTE

Lobster in Pastry Crust

You'll Need:

10 bite-size pieces cooked or
    canned lobster meat

1 package buttermilk biscuits
    Green butter

How To:

Roll out biscuits until they are flat. Put piece of lobster and pat of butter on each biscuit. Fold over, press edges together. Bake in oven according to directions on the biscuit package. Serve hot. *Serves: 6*

TOMATES AUX CREVETTES

Shrimp-Stuffed Tomatoes

You'll Need:

1 (12-ounce) package frozen,
    peeled, and cleaned shrimp
½ cup mayonnaise

½ teaspoon dry mustard
4 beautiful tomatoes,
    chilled

How To:

Cook the shrimp according to directions on the package. Cool. Mix mustard and mayonnaise. Add to shrimp. Slice the stem end of each tomato. Scoop out the inside. Fill tomato shell with shrimp mixture. Serve. *Serves: 4*

Extra Touches: Peel the tomatoes. You do this by spearing the tomato with a long-handled fork, holding it over the gas flame until the skin blisters and cracks. Then it's a snap to peel off the skin. Or dip tomatoes in scalding hot water, let stand 1 minute, drain, and skin. Diced hard-cooked egg yolk looks nice sprinkled on top of each tomato. But if you don't have hard-cooked egg yolk handy, there is always parsley or chives. Chop fine and sprinkle on each stuffed tomato.

S A U C I S S O N S

Cold Cuts

Buy 3 or 4 different kinds of ready-to-serve cold cuts. Put a slice of each on individual plates. Serve with crusty French bread and sweet butter.

Some interesting sausages that come from the Italian markets are mortadella, cotechino, capocollo, and salami. Mortadella and cotechino are about the size and shape of a wide bologna. They are delicious! Capocollo looks like Canadian bacon with an orange rim. The orange rim is red pepper. A slice of each of the above, plus a slice of Genoa salami, would make a wonderful first course.

Extra Touches: If you choose a Genoa salami, ask to have it cut slantwise across the roll so that the slices are oval rather than round. If you choose a sweet sausage that is shaped like a foot-long hot dog, have it sliced vertically, so that you have very long thin slices. A variety of shapes, as well as a variety of flavors, makes the platter more interesting.

COEUR A LA CREME

Cream Cheese with Cherry Tomatoes and Onions

You'll Need:

1 (3-ounce) package cream
cheese
1 heart-shaped cookie cutter

6 cherry tomatoes
4 black olives
2 green onions (scallions)

How To:

Cut cheese into a heart shape. Put on small plate and surround with cherry tomatoes, green onions and black olives.
If cherry tomatoes are out of season, radishes will do. Serve
with thin slices of brown bread and butter. *Serves: 2*

ASPERGES FRANCAISES

Hot Asparagus

You'll Need:

1 (No. 2) can white asparagus
1 (½-pint) jar Hollandaise

sauce
1 teaspoon lemon juice.

How To:

Heat asparagus. Drain. Arrange on warm platter. Heat
Hollandaise sauce in double boiler over boiling water, add
lemon juice a few drops at a time stirring constantly. Remove as soon as sauce is hot. It must not boil. *Serves: 4*

Extra Touches: Buy a jar of the extra-long white imported
asparagus, and 2 jars of Hollandaise sauce.

ARTICHAUTS FROIDS

Cold Artichokes with Caviar

You'll Need:

2 cooked and cooled artichokes (with choke removed)	½ pint sour cream ½-ounce jar red or pressed black caviar

How To:

Fill center of each cold artichoke with sour cream. Top with caviar. Serve each artichoke on a folded white napkin on a small plate. *Serves: 2*

Note: There's no way out of it. You have to cook your own artichokes this time. But you can do it the day before. That's a help. Trim the sharp points off the artichoke leaves with scissors. Grab the stem and push the artichoke against your work table to spread the leaves apart and allow you to reach the choke. Cut out the choke. Cook artichokes for 20 minutes in boiling, salted water to cover, or until tender. Drain and chill.

Extra Touches: This is more than an extra touch. This is another dish: Artichokes stuffed with crab meat. Forget about the sour cream and caviar. Fill the cooked and chilled artichokes with crab meat. Top with a sauce made by combining the following ingredients: ⅔ cup mayonnaise, ⅓ cup chili sauce, 1 teaspoon lemon juice, 1 tablespoon chopped chives, 1 tablespoon chopped parsley, 2 tablespoons pickle relish. *Serves: 2*

CROQUE MADAME

Brioche Ham-and-Cheese Sandwich

You'll Need:

6 brioches   6 slices Swiss cheese
                   6 slices boiled ham

How To:

Slice brioches crosswise, a little thicker than you would
slice bread. Make neat ham-and-cheese sandwiches. (A
cookie cutter will help you cut the cheese and ham neatly.)
You should have 12 sandwiches. Bake in 400° oven for
5 minutes. *Serves: 6 or 12*

FONDUE SUISSE

Swiss Cheese Fondue with Kirsch

You'll Need:

1 package refrigerated Swiss   Small loaf French bread cut
  Knight Fondue   in 2-inch cubes. (One loaf
1 ounce (2 tablespoons)   of brown-and-serve French
  kirsch   bread of the variety that
1 canned white truffle, sliced   comes 2 loaves in a package)

How To:

Heat cheese according to directions on the package. Add
kirsch and sliced truffle. Serve in individual earthenware
casseroles. Surround with small chunks of bread. Eat the
fondue by spearing bread with a fork and dipping it into
the hot cheese. The principle is the same as mopping up
gravy. *Serves: 2*

Extra Touches: Make a lot. Serve cheese mixture in a chafing dish in the center of the table with a basket of bread. When cheese is melted, kirsch and truffle added, set the chafing-dish pan on the lower pan containing hot water. Give everyone a long-handled kitchen fork to spear the bread. This eating out of a community pot is very chummy and is nice for an after-theater party.

CELERI REMOULADE

Celery Rémoulade

If you ever run into celery root, scrub this vegetable, then peel and sliver like shoe-string potatoes. Soak in cold salted water a few hours. Mix with rémoulade sauce. Serve on lettuce as appetizer.

SOUPS

POTAGE PUREE DE POIS

POTAGE GRAND DUC

POTAGE CREME DE CRESSON

CREME D'EPINARD

BORSCHT

POTAGE CREME D'ASPERGE

POTAGE AU TOMATE

VICHYSSOISE

SOUPE A L'OIGNON

CONSOMME AUX CHAMPIGNONS

SOUPE AU FROMAGE

POTAGE CRECY

GAZPACHO

CONSOMME BELLEVUE

BOULA BOULA

POTAGE A LA TORTUE

BISQUE DE CREVETTES GARNI HOMARD

SOUPE AUX PALOURDES

SOUPE AUX MOULES

CONSOMME MELANGE

POTAGE CINGALAISE

The Good Soup

To the French a dinner without soup is unthinkable. In fact, some meals *are* soup. Bouillabaisse is soup at heart. Still, the soup course seems the right place to economize on time. With all the slow simmered canned soups you find — or boxed or frozen — at your supermarket, you might as well take advantage of the time the packers have spent for you. A famous chef I met, a friend of Escoffier, said to me that no one struggles to make a good turtle soup anymore. When he was a boy, he started with the turtle. Now he starts with a can. And, he added thoughtfully, he couldn't really tell the difference in the finished soup. I left him in a quiet mood. I had a similar experience with fresh cream of tomato soup versus the canned variety. We both had our private thoughts.

Cold Curried Pea Soup

You'll Need:

1 (10½-ounce) can condensed
  cream of pea soup
½ soup can milk
½ soup can light cream

1 teaspoon, or more, curry
  powder
2 tablespoons cooked frozen
  peas

How To:

Combine all ingredients except peas. Beat with an egg beater.
Chill. Pour into cups. Garnish each cup with a teaspoonful
of peas. *Serves: 2 or 3*

POTAGE GRAND DUC

Cream of Cauliflower Soup

You'll Need:

1 (10-ounce) can frozen
  cream of potato soup
1½ soup cans milk
1 teaspoon dry mustard
3 tablespoons butter

1 (10-ounce) package frozen
  cauliflower, cooked
1 tablespoon fresh cut or
  frozen chopped chives
  Croutons

How To:

Add milk, mustard, and butter to soup and heat just to
boiling point. Add cauliflower. Stir until mixture is hot.
Strain. Reheat. Add chives. Serve with croutons. *Serves: 4*

POTAGE CREME DE CRESSON
Cream of Watercress Soup

You'll Need:

2 (10-ounce) cans frozen cream of potato soup
2 soup cans milk
4 tablespoons butter

1 cup watercress, coarsely chopped
2 tablespoons chopped watercress reserved for garnish

How To:

Combine soup, milk, butter, and all but a little of the watercress and bring slowly to the boiling point. Scorching is a hazard, so keep stirring all the time. When just ready to boil, remove from heat, and strain. Serve in soup bowls, using watercress to garnish each serving. *Serves: 5 or 6*

Extra Touches: You can substitute 1 small head shredded romaine lettuce for the watercress and call it Crème de Romaine.

CREME D'EPINARD
Cream of Spinach Soup

You'll Need:

1 (13¾-ounce) can chicken broth
1 jar chopped green spinach

(baby food, junior size)
Croutons

How To:

Heat soup and spinach together, but do not boil. Serve at once. Pass hot croutons. *Serves: 2*

BORSCHT
Beet Soup

You'll Need:

1 (10½-ounce) can con-
densed beef bouillon
1 (10-ounce) jar strained
beets (baby food)

½ teaspoon celery salt or
seasoning salt
Juice of ½ lemon
Sour cream

How To:

Combine and heat all ingredients except sour cream. Serve
in cups with a spoonful of sour cream floating on the top of
each cup. *Serves: 2 or 3*

Extra Touches: Jellied Borscht: Substitute beef consommé
for beef bouillon. Combine ingredients and chill. To serve,
top with sour cream.

POTAGE CREME D'ASPERGE
Cream of Asparagus Soup

You'll Need:

1 bunch fresh green onions
(scallions)
1 cup canned chicken broth
1 (10½-ounce) can condensed

cream of asparagus soup
1 small can white asparagus
tips
Heaping teaspoon butter

How To:

Chop onions, tops and all. Cook in chicken broth until tender. Add asparagus soup. Heat. Strain. Return to pot. Add
only the tip ends of the canned white asparagus tips and
the butter. Make sure soup is hot but do not boil. Serve at
once. *Serves: 2 or 3*

POTAGE AU TOMATE

Cream of Tomato Soup with Dill

You'll Need:

2 (10½-ounce) cans con-
densed cream of tomato
soup
1 (13¾-ounce) can chicken
broth
1 tomato, peeled and chopped
1 tablespoon chopped fresh

dill (if dill is unavailable,
dried or fresh parsley or
frozen or fresh chopped
chives will do)
1 tablespoon cream for each
serving

How To:

Heat soups together. Add tomato and dill or other herb and
just heat through. Float a tablespoon of cream on top of
each serving. *Serves: 3 or 4*

VICHYSSOISE

Cold Potato and Leek Soup

You'll Need:

1 (10-ounce) can frozen
vichyssoise
½ cup milk
½ cup canned chicken broth

1 teaspoon dry mustard
2 tablespoons light cream
1 tablespoon frozen chopped
chives

How To:

Prepare soup according to directions on the can, using the
milk and chicken broth. Season with dry mustard. Put in
electric blender about 1 minute or through a strainer. Chill.
Just before serving, add cream and mix well. Pour into
chilled soup cups. Top with chives. *Serves: 2 or 3*

SOUPE A L'OIGNON
Onion Soup

You'll Need:

1 (10½-ounce) can condensed onion soup
¾ soup can water
3 tablespoons grated Swiss cheese

3 slices French bread, toasted
3 pats (or tablespoons) butter
3 teaspoons grated Parmesan cheese

How To:

Mix soup and water. Ladle into three individual earthenware casseroles. Put tablespoon of Swiss cheese in each, slice of toast, pat of butter, and teaspoon of Parmesan cheese. Heat about 10 minutes in a moderate oven, or until soup is hot and cheese is melted. *Serves: 3*

CONSOMME AUX CHAMPIGNONS
Beef Broth with Mushrooms

You'll Need:

4 mushrooms (select nice white ones so you don't have to peel them)
Lemon juice

1 (13¾-ounce) can beef broth
1 teaspoon chopped parsley, dill or chives

How To:

Wash mushrooms, drain, slice or dice thinly. Cover with lemon juice. Let sit for 5 minutes. Add lemon juice-mushroom mixture to the beef broth. Heat, but do not boil. Sprinkle with chopped herb and serve. *Serves: 2 or 3*

SOUPE AU FROMAGE
Cheese Soup
You'll Need:

1 (10-ounce) can condensed
cheese soup
1 soup can milk
1 egg
2 tablespoons butter

1 tablespoon shredded Cheddar cheese
Paprika
Buttered toast

How To:

Combine soup, milk, and yolk of egg, beating with a whisk over low heat. Heat, but don't boil. Add butter and cheese. Stir about 1 minute, and serve at once. Pour into soup bowls. Sprinkle with paprika. Serve with rounds of buttered toast. *Serves: 2 or 3*

POTAGE CRECY
Cream of Carrot Soup
You'll Need:

1 (10-ounce) can frozen
cream of potato soup
1 cup canned chicken broth
1 jar chopped carrots (baby
food, junior size)

1 tablespoon butter
3 tablespoons cream
1 teaspoon chopped parsley
Dash red cayenne pepper

How To:

Prepare potato soup according to directions on package, using chicken broth as the liquid. Strain. Return to pot. Add rest of the ingredients all at once. Stir and heat, but do not boil. Serve at once. *Serves: 3*

GAZPACHO
Iced Salad Soup

You'll Need:

1 (10-ounce) can tomato juice

1 (10-ounce) can mixed vegetable juices

1 teaspoon garlic juice

3 tablespoons olive oil

3 tablespoons red wine vinegar

4 tablespoons frozen chopped onions

6 tablespoons frozen chopped green pepper

6 tomatoes, peeled and sliced or cubed

1 small jar pitted green olives (drained)

1 teaspoon salt

Dash of black pepper

8 ice cubes

How To:

Combine all ingredients except the ice cubes in a bowl. Mix thoroughly. Season to taste. Add the ice cubes. Place in refrigerator until read to serve. Then serve in soup plates. *Serves: 4*

Extra Touches: Some garnishes you might like to try: a tablespoon of cold, cooked rice in each bowl; one-inch cubes of toasted garlic bread; tablespoon of sour cream in each bowl.

CONSOMME BELLEVUE
Clam and Chicken Broth

Combine equal amounts of canned clam juice and canned chicken broth or bouillon. Heat. Top each serving with sour cream or plain unseasoned whipped cream. Sprinkle with chopped parsley.

BOULA BOULA

Turtle and Pea Soup

You'll Need:

1 (No. 2½) can green turtle
  consommé
1 (10½-ounce) can condensed
  pea soup
½ cup light cream

⅛ teaspoon curry powder
½ teaspoon marjoram
⅛ teaspoon aniseed
1 small piece bay leaf,
  crumbled fine

How To:

Combine the soups and seasoning in a sauce pan. Heat, adding cream. Pour at once into individual earthenware casseroles. Float a tablespoon of cream in each casserole, and brown lightly under moderate broiler heat. *Serves: 4*, unless you use extra large soup bowls.

Extra Touches: Sprinkle with grated Parmesan cheese and place under broiler heat until lightly browned.

POTAGE A LA TORTUE

Turtle Soup

You'll Need:

1 (1 pint, 3½ ounce) can
  turtle soup

2 teaspoons sherry

How To:

Add sherry to the soup. Heat but do not boil. Serve. Pass more sherry. *Serves: 2*

BISQUE DE CREVETTES GARNI HOMARD

Shrimp and Lobster Bisque

You'll Need:

1 (10-ounce) can frozen cream of shrimp soup
Pinch of saffron powder

Pinch or two of paprika
3 tablespoons lobster meat

How To:

Prepare shrimp soup according to directions on package. Strain. Return to pot. Season with saffron. Color with paprika. Make sure soup is hot, but do not boil. Garnish with lobster meat. Serve at once. *Serves: 2*

Extra Touches: This soup is good cold too.

SOUPE AUX PALOURDES

Clam Bisque

You'll Need:

1 (10½-ounce) can condensed cream of celery soup
1 (7½-ounce) can minced clams

½ cup canned chicken broth or bouillon
½ cup light cream

How To:

Combine all ingredients. Heat, but do not boil. Serve at once. *Serves: 3*

Extra Touches: For Oyster Bisque omit canned clams. Substitute a dozen small raw oysters and their juice.

SOUPE AUX MOULES

Cold Mussel Soup

You'll Need:

1 (12-ounce) can cream of onion soup (not condensed)
9 mussels (canned)
1 teaspoon mussel juice from the can
3 tablespoons cream
Pinch of saffron

How To:

Pour soup through a coarse sieve. Heat soup slowly, but do not let it boil. Add all other ingredients. Mix and remove from heat. Chill. Serve in iced cups. Make sure each serving contains at least 3 mussels. *Serves: 2*

CONSOMME MELANGE

Chicken and Beef Broth

You'll Need:

1 (13¾-ounce) can chicken broth
1 (13-ounce) can beef broth
1 tablespoon julienne canned carrots
1 tablespoon sliced celery
4 rounds toasted French bread
4 tablespoons grated Parmesan cheese

How To:

Heat soup and vegetables. Make toast. To serve, put a piece of toast in bottom of each soup plate. Pour hot soup over it. Pass cheese. *Serves: 4*

POTAGE CINGALAISE

Cold Curried Cream of Chicken Soup

How To:

Mix 1 (10½-ounce) can of condensed cream of chicken soup with soup can of milk and a teaspoon of curry powder. Chill. *Serves: 2*

FISH

LANGOUSTE A L'ARMORICAINE
FILET DE SOLE AMANDINE
BOUILLABAISSE
MOULES BLANCHES
MOUSSE DE SAUMON
TRUITE AU BLEU EN GELEE
MOULES A LA POULETTE
HUITRES EN EPINARD
MOULES AU CURRY
ESCARGOTS A LA BOURGUIGNONNE
TRUITE AU BLEU
GRENOUILLES SAUTEES A LA PROVENCALE
SALADE NICOISE
CREVETTES AU CURRY
QUENELLES DE BROCHET
SCAMPI

Fish

A steamed trout can be as delightful a main course as an entrecôte. And large numbers of people would choose bouillabaisse over hamburger.

If you still hesitate, let me hurry to say that these fish dishes are no more difficult to prepare than a hamburger. The most difficult part of fish cookery used to be getting the fish ready for the pan. But when you get your trout out of the freezer, rather than out of the river, and your snails out of a can, rather than fresh, your biggest worries are over. The other difficulty is the problem of getting fresh fish. If you haven't a house by the sea or on a river, the freezer and the pantry shelf are fine substitutes.

LANGOUSTE A L'ARMORICAINE

Lobster in Tomato Sauce with Brandy

You'll Need:

6 (4-6 ounce) frozen lobster
tails
3 tablespoons vegetable oil
3 tablespoons frozen chopped
onions
¼ cup brandy
1 cup white wine
2 teaspoons tomato paste
¾ cup beef broth

2 bouillon cubes (or 2
teaspoons Bovril)
3 fresh tomatoes, or canned
equivalents cut in eighths
¼ teaspoon saffron
2 tablespoons beurre manié
Salt
Pepper

How To:

Heat oil in large frying pan. Thaw lobster tails and split in
half lengthwise and place in pan, meat side down. Cook for
a few minutes. Turn, cook some more. The shell will turn
red. Add onions. Cook till they turn yellow, but don't
brown them. Add brandy. When warm, ignite brandy
with a match; it will flame up, so turn your face away.
When the flame dies, add all the rest of the ingredients except the beurre manié (the butter-flour mixture). Cover
the pot and let cook slowly for ½ hour. Add butter-flour
mixture bit by bit and stir to thicken sauce. Taste and add
salt and pepper if needed. *Serves: 3 to 6*

Extra Touches: Anything more would be showy.

FILET DE SOLE AMANDINE

Fillet of Sole with Almonds

You'll Need:

1 (12-ounce) package frozen cooked fish (sole or flounder) fillets

¼ pound butter
½ cup canned blanched and slivered almonds

How To:

Cook fish according to directions on package. Meanwhile melt butter. Add almonds. Stir and heat till brown. Pour this sauce over the fish and place back in the oven for a few minutes. *Serves: 3*

Extra Touches: Garnish with parsley or watercress and lemon wedges dusted with paprika.

BOUILLABAISSE

Fish Stew

You'll Need:

1 tablespoon butter
1 teaspoon frozen chopped onions
1 cup canned stewed tomatoes
½ cup white wine
½ cup juice from can of canned clams
Saffron
Clove garlic, peeled

Pepper
1 small sea bass, cleaned and cut in half (or other fresh fish)
10 clams in shell (canned)
¼ pound lobster meat (canned, frozen, or fresh cooked)
1 teaspoon chopped parsley
2 slices French bread, toasted in broiler

How To:

Cook onions in butter till golden. Add tomatoes, wine, clam juice, saffron, garlic, and pepper. Cook for a few minutes. Add sea bass. Cook 8 minutes. Add clams and lobster. Cook just long enough to heat. Sprinkle with parsley. Serve in soup plates, with a slice of toasted French bread in each plate. *Serves: 2*

MOULES BLANCHES

Mussels in White Celery Sauce

You'll Need:

4 tablespoons butter (½ stick)
1 cup dry white wine
Dash of white pepper
Sprig of parsley
2 tablespoons frozen chopped onions

Pinch of thyme
½ cup canned condensed cream of celery soup
2 (9-ounce) cans mussels, drained
2 slices toasted French bread

How To:

Combine 2 tablespoons of butter, the wine, pepper, parsley, onions, thyme, and soup in a pan and stir and cook 5 minutes. Remove the parsley. Add the mussels and just heat through. Add the remaining 2 tablespoons of butter, bit by bit, and the parsley, again. Serve at once. *Serves: 2*

Extra Touches: Serve in soup bowls with a thick slice of toasted French bread in each bowl.

MOUSSE DE SAUMON

Cold Salmon Mousse

You'll Need:

1 (No. 1) can tomato madrilène

1 envelope (1 tablespoon) unflavored gelatin

1 black truffle, or 6 black olives, sliced

1 (7-ounce) can salmon

4 tablespoons mayonnaise

Juice ½ lemon

Salt

Pepper

Watercress

How To:

Put the gelatin in the madrilène, and heat until gelatin is dissolved. Pour enough gelatin mixture into the bottom of a one-quart mold to line the bottom. Place mold in refrigerator until gelatin is egg-white consistency. Or place it in freezer for just a minute. Then decorate with thin slices of truffle or black olives. Place the olive slices so that the black shiny skin will show when you turn the mold out. Put the mold back in the refrigerator to become firm. Mash the salmon with a fork. Remove any bones. Add lemon juice to mayonnaise and add to salmon. Mash some more. Taste, add salt and pepper as needed. Pile salmon mixture into the mold leaving some room around all sides. Pour the remaining gelatin around the edges. Place in refrigerator to become firm, then turn out on a bed of watercress. *Serves: 3 to 4*

Extra Touches: Serve with cold rice salad. Use a mold that is shaped like a fish. Decorate with the sliced black truffle *and* bits of lobster meat.

TRUITE AU BLEU EN GELEE

Trout in Aspic

You'll Need:

3 (8-ounce) bottles (3 cups) clam juice

2 tablespoons white-wine vinegar

1 package frozen rainbow trout (each package con-

tains 2 trout) defrosted

1 envelope (1 tablespoon) unflavored gelatin

1 canned black truffle, sliced

Watercress

Pimiento

How To:

Combine the clam juice and vinegar and bring to a boil. Put the trout in the pot. Cover. Turn the heat low and simmer for 8 minutes. Soften gelatin in ½ cup cold water. Dissolve in 1½ cups of the hot liquid the fish cooked in. Peel skin off fish with your fingers (but leave the head and tail intact). Put fish on platter to cool, and let the gelatin cool till it has the consistency of raw egg white. Coat the fish with the gelatin. Decorate with sliced black truffles and red pimiento strips that have been dipped into the gelatin mixture. Let remaining gelatin harden on another plate. When it's good and hard, chop it with a knife. Surround the fish with the chopped gelatin and some watercress. Serve very cold. *Serves: 2*

MOULES A LA POULETTE

Mussels in Golden Sauce

You'll Need:

2 (9-ounce) cans mussels
1¼ cups canned chicken
   gravy
   Juice ½ lemon
2 tablespoons butter
   Cayenne pepper

1 tablespoon chopped, dried
   parsley
1 egg yolk, beaten slightly
1 or 2 tablespoons chopped,
   fresh parsley

How To:

Drain can of mussels. Reserve juice. Put chicken gravy in pot to heat with ¼ cup of mussel juice, and the lemon juice. Add butter bit by bit, a dash of cayenne pepper, the dried parsley, and egg yolk. Stir all the time using a wire whisk. Keep the heat low. Add the mussels. Cook only until they are heated through. Sprinkle with fresh parsley. Serve in a ring of hot rice. *Serves: 6*

Extra Touches: A bib lettuce or watercress salad would be the right light touch.

Call it Fruits de la Mer: substitute 1 (7-ounce) package of frozen shrimp for 1 can mussels. Cook shrimp before adding.

Pot Note: Mussels are a favorite of mine; and I'm lucky that my grocer always has them in stock. If they are not available near your home, substitute clams (canned) in all the mussel recipes in the book. They are equally easy — and delicious.

HUITRES EN EPINARD

Oysters Rockefeller

You'll Need:

1 (12-ounce) package frozen
  chopped spinach
4 tablespoons (½ stick) sweet
  butter

2 tablespoons sour cream
Salt
Pepper
1 dozen large oysters

How To:

Cook spinach until it is just barely done. Drain well, stir in half the butter, all the sour cream, and season. Place in 2 or 3 small shallow casseroles and arrange oysters on top. Dot with remaining butter and season with coarse-ground pepper. Place under moderate broiler heat for a few minutes until oysters curl. They should be heated through but still plump. Serve with toast points or croutons. *Serves: 2 or 3*

MOULES AU CURRY

Mussels in Curry Sauce

You'll Need:

2 (9-ounce) cans mussels
1 (10½-ounce) can condensed

cream of chicken soup
1½ teaspoons curry powder

How To:

Combine chicken soup and curry. Heat till bubbly. Add drained mussels. Just heat through. Serve at once in a ring of hot rice. *Serves: 4 to 5*

Extra Touches: Add chopped parsley as garnish.

ESCARGOTS A LA BOURGUIGNONNE

Burgundy Snails

You'll Need:

1 can snails with shells* (24 in a can)
½ pound sweet butter
2 tablespoons chopped shallots or 2 tablespoons chopped onions
2 cloves garlic, squeezed through a garlic press, or chopped fine
2 tablespoons chopped parsley
Pinch of pepper
½ cup white wine

How To:

Mix all the ingredients except snails together with a fork. Put a little of this flavored butter in each shell. Then put a snail in the shell. Then put more of the butter mixture on top of the snail in the shell. Bake the snails in a 350° oven until they are hot and the butter is bubbly. Baste from time to time with white wine. *Serves: 2 to 4.* Some people can eat 12. Most servings consist of 6 snails.

Extra Touches: You can be fancy and buy special tools for snails. A snail plate is about the size of a salad plate. It has little round depressions that just accommodate a snail shell. Since it is made of metal, you can also use this dish for baking. Each plate comes with a little pair of tongs and a cocktail fork so that you can hold the shell firmly with the tongs and pry the snail out with the fork. But none of this is as important as some good crusty bread to mop up all the butter sauce.

* Shells come separate in a container attached to the can, and can be re-used. One brand comes with 2 baking dishes and shells packed in can.

TRUITE AU BLEU

Trout in Butter Sauce

You'll Need:

3 (8-ounce) bottles clam
  juice
2 tablespoons white-wine
  vinegar
1 package frozen rainbow

trout (package contains
  2 trout), defrosted
3 or or 4 tablespoons butter,
  melted

How To:

Combine the clam juice and vinegar and heat to a boil. Add
the trout to the pot. Cover. Turn heat low. Simmer for 8
minutes. Remove fish, and serve with melted butter.
Serves: 2

Extra Touches: The trout is best served with plain melted
butter and plain boiled potatoes. You can buy frozen small
new potatoes that are peeled and partly cooked, saving still
more time. If you want to dress it up, peel the skin off the
cooked trout with your fingers, and garnish with pimiento
strips and chives. Serve on fresh dill.

Perhaps you are surprised that the fish is complete with
head and tail. Swallow your surprise. It's supposed to be
served that way.

Pot Note: A good way to cook fish is to place the fish on a
rack in a roasting pan. Add about 1 inch water to the pan,
cover, and steam fish until tender. The boiling water should
not touch the fish. It is easier to get the fish onto the platter
without breaking it, because you simply lift the rack and
slide the fish onto the platter.

GRENOUILLES SAUTEES A LA PROVENCALE

Frogs Legs in Tomato and Garlic Sauce

You'll Need:

4 tablespoons butter
4 pairs frozen frogs legs
Flour or fine dry crumbs

1 cup canned marinara sauce
1 tablespoon chopped fresh
parsley

How To:

Melt the butter in a frying pan. Dust the frogs legs with flour or fine dry crumbs. Cook gently until legs are browned on all sides. Remove to heated serving dish and add the marinara sauce to the pan. Stir and heat. Pour over frogs legs. Sprinkle with parsley and serve. *Serves: 2*

Extra Touches: Artichoke hearts would look nice on the plate. Cook a package of frozen ones according to directions on the package. Drain, add butter and more of that chopped parsley.

SALADE NICOISE

Niçoise Salad

You'll Need:

1 (No. 2) can sliced potatoes
1 (12-ounce) package frozen
French-cut green beans,
cooked and cooled
½ cup bottled herb salad
dressing

3 fresh tomatoes, peeled and
cut in eighths
1 (7-ounce) can tuna fish
2 small bottles anchovies
rolled with capers
1 (14-ounce) can pitted black
olives

How To:

Mix the drained potatoes and drained green beans with herb dressing. Pile in the center of a wooden salad bowl. Make a border around the potatoes and beans with the tomatoes. Crumble the tuna fish over the bean and potato mixture. Arrange anchovies on top of tuna fish. Place the olives in a ring between the tomatoes and the tuna fish. *Serves: 4 well or 6 meagerly.*

Extra Touches: Serve ice-cold with hot French bread. Pass the pepper mill. Or the pepper shaker.

CREVETTES AU CURRY

Shrimp in Curry Sauce

You'll Need:

2 (12-ounce) packages frozen peeled and cleaned shrimp
1 (10½-ounce) can condensed cream of chicken soup
1½ teaspoons curry powder

How To:

Cook the shrimp according to directions on the package. Drain. Heat soup. Stir in curry. Add the cooked shrimps. Serve at once. *Serves: 6*

Extra Touches: Well . . . some people like curry with a lot of extras. Let's settle for mounds of rice and chutney.

QUENELLES DE BROCHET

Fish Quenelles in Shrimp Sauce

You'll Need:

1 (14-ounce) jar gefilte fish balls (or regular)
1 (10-ounce) can frozen condensed shrimp soup
½ soup can cream (or white wine)

How To:

Defrost soup in the refrigerator. Mix soup and cream or wine in a shallow casserole. Add drained fish dumplings, coating them with the sauce. Heat in a moderate (350°) oven until bubbly. *Serves: 2 as a main dish at lunch.*

Extra Touches: Decorate with small whole cooked shrimp, bits of lobster, or king crab in the shell. Sprinkle with parsley. Surround with buttered toast points, if you like.

SCAMPI

Broiled Shrimp

You'll Need:

2 pounds fresh large shrimp
  Vegetable oil
  Salt

Garlic salt or finely
chopped peeled garlic

How To:

Spread shrimp out on a flat baking tin so that all 2 pounds of them lie flat. Brush with oil and dust with salt and garlic salt. Broil until shells turn pink — which should be within 5 minutes. Turn shrimp once so that both sides are pink. *Serves: 6*

Extra Touches: Since the shrimp are eaten with the finger, serve with lots of paper napkins.

MEAT

ESCALOPES DE VEAU AUX CHAMPIGNONS
BLANQUETTE DE VEAU
GIGOT D'AGNEAU AUX HARICOTS
GIGOT D'AGNEAU EN CROUTE
CERVELLES DE VEAU AU BEURRE NOIR
FOIE DE VEAU A L'ORANGE
RIS DE VEAU MARSALA
RIS DE VEAU PERIGOURDINE
BOEUF BRAISE
BOEUF BRAISE DU BARRY
COTELETTES D'AGNEAU IRWIN
FONDUE BOURGUIGNONNE
BOEUF A LA MODE
BOEUF EN GELEE
BOEUF STROGANOFF
POT AU FEU
TOURNEDOS HENRI IV
BOEUF BOURGUIGNON
ENTRECOTE AU ROQUEFORT
ENTROCOTE MIRABEAU
TOURNEDOS BEARNAISE
TOURNEDOS ROSSINI
BIFTEK MAITRE D'HOTEL
LANGUE DE BOEUF AU MADERE
LANGUE DE BOEUF AU GRATIN
JAMBON EN CROUTE
CHOUCROUTE GARNIE

Meat

How should your meat course look? As beautiful as it tastes! When the platter is passed, no one should think of the words 'hearty main course.' You should not overwhelm with quantity but with the taste with which you arrange the platter. Cook it instantly but take your time decorating and arranging it. Perhaps there will be one vegetable with the meat. The vegetable will look as though it belongs to the meat. At its best, the vegetable will be used as a garnish. No one will be able to fill up on your meat course and have to pass up the salad and dessert. Are you being skimpy? Not at all. You're being French.

The French like their meat a good deal rarer on the average than do Americans. This is especially true of lamb and chicken. If the timing given in these recipes is followed precisely, the meat will be rare. If you like your meat better done, simply increase the cooking time.

ESCALOPES DE VEAU AUX CHAMPIGNONS

Veal Scallops in Mushroom Sauce

You'll Need:

8 veal scallops or tenders
4 tablespoons (½ stick) butter
2 tablespoons frozen chopped onions
1 (3-ounce) can sliced broiled-in-butter mushrooms
½ cup white wine
½ cup beef broth
1 cup heavy cream
Chopped parsley

How To:

Have meat dealer cut scallops about ¼ inch thick. Ask him to pound them for you, or do it yourself with the edge of a plate. Heat half the butter in pan. When very hot, brown the scallops. This should take 5 minutes. Remove meat from pan. Add rest of butter. Cook onions but do not brown. Add mushrooms, wine, and broth. Add cream slowly, stirring all the time. Return meat to pan. When hot, transfer to a warmed platter. Sprinkle with chopped parsley and serve. *Serves: 4*

Extra Touches: Braised lettuce is a good vegetable to serve with veal.

Pot Note: If you know an Italian butcher, patronize his shop for your veal.

BLANQUETTE DE VEAU

Veal Stew

You'll Need:

2 pounds veal shoulder cut into 2-inch pieces
1 (10½-ounce) can condensed cream of celery soup
1 (12-ounce) can very light-colored chicken broth
1 clove
1 teaspoon salt
½ teaspoon white pepper
1 tablespoon lemon juice
1 (8-ounce) can small white onions
1 (4-ounce) can white button mushrooms
2 egg yolks
6 tablespoons cream
Chopped parsley

How To:

Cover veal with cold water and bring to a boil, and boil 3 minutes. Drain. Rinse the veal off in fresh cold water. Put the veal in another pot with celery soup and chicken broth. Add the clove. Bring to boiling, then lower the heat and cook gently for about 1 hour, or until the veal is tender. Season with salt, white pepper, and lemon juice. Add drained onions and mushrooms. To thicken sauce, beat egg yolks and cream together in a deep bowl. Pour some of the hot sauce into the bowl and beat. Pour back into the pot, stirring continually. Stir and cook about 2 minutes. Sprinkle with parsley before serving. *Serves: 6*

GIGOT D'AGNEAU AUX HARICOTS

Leg of Lamb with White Kidney Beans

You'll Need:

5-pound leg of lamb
Garlic clove
Melted butter
Crumbled dried rosemary
Coarse-ground salt

Coarse-ground pepper
2 (14-ounce) cans white
kidney beans, drained
1 tablespoon chopped parsley
or chives

How To:

Wipe meat with damp cloth. Cut slits in fat and insert bits of peeled garlic. Brush roast all over with melted butter. Season with coarse salt and pepper and rosemary. Roast uncovered in 350° oven 15 minutes per pound, for very rare, longer if you like it more well done. Let stand 10 minutes, then transfer to warmed serving platter. Gravy collects in bottom of pan. Reheat and pour over the roast. Heat drained kidney beans in some of the melted butter. Season a little with salt and pepper. Add parsley or chives for color. Slice enough lamb on the platter for one serving around the table. This should make even more gravy. Then surround with heated beans, putting them right into the gravy. Spoon some over beans and serve. *Serves: 8*

GIGOT D'AGNEAU EN CROUTE

Roast Boned Leg of Lamb in Pastry Crust

You'll Need:

2 (10-ounce) packages pie-
    crust mix
4-pound (net) leg of lamb,
    boned
Garlic salt
Salt

Pepper
¼ pound (1 stick) butter
1 teaspoon crumbled dried
    rosemary
Garlic clove
1 egg white, unbeaten

How To:

Prepare pie crust according to directions on package. Roll out so that it is double the size of the piece of lamb. Season lamb with garlic salt. Salt and pepper lamb both inside and out. Stuff hollow center with butter, rosemary, and peeled garlic clove. Sew up. Put lamb on pie crust. Fold pie crust over lamb and pinch the edges together. The lamb is now completely blanketed in pie crust. Brush with egg white. Bake uncovered in a 350° oven 15 minutes to the pound. It will be rare. That's fine. If well-done lamb is preferred, continue roasting 1 hour longer. Serve some of the brown pastry crust with each serving of meat. *Serves: 6*

CERVELLES DE VEAU AU BEURRE NOIR

Calf's Brains with Brown Butter

You'll Need:

2 pairs calf's brains
2 tablespoons lemon juice
4 tablespoons butter (½ stick)
2 teaspoons tarragon-flavored

white wine vinegar
4 tablespoons drained capers
Chopped parsley (optional)

How To:

Soak brains in cold water and half the lemon juice for 1 hour. Drain. Remove thin skin and any veins. Dry them thoroughly. Heat 2 tablespoons of the butter in a frying pan. Brown the brains on both sides, 3 minutes on each side will cook them through. Remove to warmed oven-proof platter. Keep warm in oven with the oven door slightly open. Add remaining 2 tablespoons butter to the cooking pan. Cook slowly until it turns dark brown, but not black. Add remaining lemon juice, the vinegar, and capers. Stir and pour sauce over the cooked brains, sprinkle with parsley, and serve. *Serves: 4*

FOIE DE VEAU A L'ORANGE

Calf's Liver with Orange Sauce

You'll Need:

8 very thin slices calf's liver	1 tablespoon onion juice
½ cup sifted flour	½ teaspoon garlic juice
1 teaspoon salt	1 tablespoon chopped parsley
½ teaspoon pepper	¼ cup beef broth
½ teaspoon dry mustard	¼ cup red wine
Brown paper bag	1 (11-ounce) can mandarin
4 tablespoons butter (½ stick)	orange sections, drained

How To:

Put flour and seasonings in paper bag. Put liver in bag, close tightly and shake till all is lightly coated with flour. Sauté in half the butter until golden brown. Remove liver to a warmed platter. Add all the rest of the ingredients, except the oranges, all at once. Stir and cook for 2 or 3 minutes very quickly. Stir up the brown glaze on the bottom of the pan. Add oranges, stir and just heat through. Pour this sauce over liver and serve. *Serves: 4*

RIS DE VEAU MARSALA

Sweetbreads in Marsala Sauce

You'll Need:

1 pair sweetbreads
3 tablespoons butter
1 tablespoon frozen chopped
onions

½ cup Marsala
1 teaspoon chopped dried or
fresh parsley

How To:

The day before, or 1 hour before dinner. Rinse the sweetbreads, drain, put in a pot. Cover with cold water. Bring to a boil, then lower the heat and simmer a few minutes. Drain sweetbreads and put on a plate. Place another plate on top so they are weighed down. When cool, peel off the thin skin and any tendons. Slice in half crosswise to make them thinner.

Just before dinner: Heat butter in a frying pan and brown the sweetbreads quickly. Add onions and cook till just golden. Remove sweetbreads to a warmed platter. Pour in the wine, and boil up quickly, stirring all the while. This makes a thin dark brown sauce. Pour sauce over sweetbreads. Sprinkle with parsley. Serve at once. Don't start too soon — the completed dish takes about 8 minutes to prepare. *Serves: 2*

Extra Touches: Serve on a bed of puréed peas, 4 jars of strained peas (from baby food department), heated with tablespoon butter, salt, and pepper.

RIS DE VEAU PERIGOURDINE

Sweetbreads in Madeira and Truffle Sauce

You'll Need:

2 pairs sweetbreads	½ cup canned beef broth
4 tablespoons (½ stick) butter	½ cup Madeira
½ cup beef gravy	1 or 2 truffles, sliced

How To:

Before: Place sweetbreads in cold water and bring to a boil. Remove sweetbreads from pot. Drain. Cool between two plates so that the sweetbreads are weighed down. When they are cool enough to handle, peel off the thin skin and remove any tendons. Slice each sweetbread in half crosswise to make them thinner. You'll now have 8 pieces of meat ready for the pan.

At dinnertime: Heat butter in a frying pan. Brown sweetbreads quickly, 3 minutes on each side will cook them nicely. Remove the cooked sweetbreads to a warmed platter. Add the rest of the ingredients to the pan, stirring as you pour them in. Stir and boil for 3 minutes. Pour sauce over sweetbreads and serve at once. *Serves: 4*

Extra Touches: Heat package of frozen rissolé potatoes. Put on platter with sweetbreads. Pour sauce over all.

BOEUF BRAISE

Braised Beef in Onion Soup

You'll Need:

1 pot roast of beef weighing about 3¼ pounds (the bottom of the round is a nice cut for this dish)

3 tablespoons flour mixed with

1 teaspoon salt

1 (1¾-ounce) package dehydrated onion soup

¼ cup boiling water (optional)

How To:

Brown meat in its own fat in a heavy pot or Dutch oven. Add onion soup and boiling water. Cover tightly. Simmer till done, about 2½ to 3 hours. Turn the roast twice during cooking period. If your pot lid is really tight, you won't need a drop more of water. The meat will make its own juice. *Serves: 4*

Extra Touches: Add 8 frozen potatoes peeled and partly cooked during the last half hour of cooking.

BOEUF BRAISE DU BARRY

Braised Beef Garnished with Cauliflower

You'll Need:

3½-pound boneless pot roast (sirloin tip, eye round, top of the round)

1 teaspoon salt

2 cups red wine

1¼ cups canned beef gravy

1 teaspoon chopped fresh basil or parsley

2 (12-ounce) packages frozen cauliflower

4 tablespoons (½ stick) butter

2 tablespoons grated Parmesan cheese

How To:

Salt and brown beef in its own fat in a heavy pot or Dutch oven. Combine red wine, gravy, and basil, and pour it over the meat. Cover. Reduce heat to a simmer. Cook on top of stove about 3 hours (or in a 350° oven for the same amount of time). Cook cauliflower according to directions on the package. Drain. Add butter to cauliflower. Slice the meat and arrange on an oven-proof platter. Pour the sauce in which it has cooked over the meat. Pile cooked cauliflower on either end. Sprinkle cheese on cauliflower. Place platter under moderate broiler heat till cauliflower is light brown and sauce bubbles. *Serves: 6*

COTELETTES D'AGNEAU IRWIN

Breaded Lamb Chops with Tomato Sauce

You'll Need:

4 single-cut rib lamb chops	Garlic clove
1 egg, beaten lightly	Vegetable oil
½ cup bread crumbs	1 (8-ounce) can tomato sauce

How To:

Wipe chops with damp cloth. Dip chops in egg, then bread crumbs. Sauté quickly in hot oil with peeled garlic, 3 minutes on each side will do it, or longer if preferred. Remove garlic and discard. Heat tomato sauce just as it comes from the can, and pour it over chops. Serve at once. *Serves: 2*

Extra Touches: Heat French-fried zucchini and French-fried eggplant in the oven, according to directions on their packages. Surround chops with these vegetables and pour tomato sauce over all.

FONDUE BOURGUIGNONNE

Beef Fondue

You'll Need:

A chafing dish or an
electric fry pan
Vegetable oil
4 long forks*

1½ pounds steak, cubed into
1-inch pieces, seasoned with
salt and pepper
Assorted sauces

How To:

Pour 2 inches of oil into the chafing dish or electric fry pan. Heat so that it bubbles. Keep it hot throughout the meal. Guests spear a cube of raw meat with their long cooking forks and cook it to rare, medium, or well done. They dip meat in the sauce of their choice. Eat it, and start all over again. Small individual sauce dishes are grouped around each guest's plate. *Serves: 4*

Some Garnish Suggestions:

Toasted slivered almonds
Chopped tomatoes
Parsley and chives

Cold mushroom with dill
Pickles and olives
Matchstick potatoes

Some Sauce Suggestions:

Hot Béarnaise
Cold curry mayonnaise
Chili sauce (out of the bottle)
Cocktail sauce (chili sauce
  with horse-radish with

chopped chives)
Mayonnaise with capers and
  lemon juice
Sour cream Béarnaise

---

* You can buy Bourguignonne sets. They come with 2 forks per person, 1 to cook with and 1 to eat with.

BOEUF A LA MODE

Braised Beef in Red Wine

You'll Need:

5-pound rump roast
1 bottle dry red wine
1 (10½-ounce) can beef
  broth
1¼ cups canned beef gravy

1 (No. 1) can tiny carrots
1 (No. 1) can tiny whole
  onions
2 tablespoons port

How To:

Pour wine over the roast and let stand about 6 hours. Turn the meat several times during this marinating period. This is an optional step, but adds flavor. Drain the beef, and dry thoroughly with paper towels. Then brown it in a heavy pot or Dutch oven on top of the stove. If the meat hasn't enough fat, cover the top of the roast with bacon. Take meat out of the pot. Pour half the red wine in which the meat has been marinating into the pot. Cook rapidly for a few minutes. Add beef broth and gravy. Return meat to pot, cover, and cook in a 350° oven for 3 or 4 hours or until done. Transfer the pot to the top of the stove. Add carrots, onions, and port, continue cooking until vegetables are hot. Serve meat on warmed platter with vegetables and pot gravy.
Serves: 6

Pot Note: This dish spends 3 hours in the oven. But you don't have to spend more than 15 minutes in the kitchen. And it's *your* time we're saving.

BOEUF EN GELEE

Cold Roast Beef in Aspic

You'll Need:

5-pound "eye" of the round beef
Salt
Pepper
1 tablespoon frozen chopped onions
2 envelopes (2 tablespoons) unflavored gelatin

3 cups beef broth
¼ cup port
1 (8-ounce) can tiny whole carrots
1 (8-ounce) can tiny whole onions
Watercress for garnish

How To:

Salt and pepper the meat. Place in uncovered roasting pan, scatter onions on top, and roast uncovered at 350°; it should take 1½ hours for a very rare roast. Allow 27 minutes a pound for medium-rare roast, 33 minutes a pound for well done. When the meat is done, let it cool. Juices will gather in the bottom of the pan. Slice the meat. Dissolve the gelatin in the beef broth, and add port and every drop of meat juice from the pan. Arrange the sliced meat in a large mold with the drained carrots and onions. Pour the gelatin mixture over the meat. Set the mold in the refrigerator. You should have more of the gelatin mixture than you need to cover the meat and vegetables. Pour what is left into a square pan and place it in the refrigerator. To serve, turn the chilled, set mold out on a cold platter decorated with watercress. Chop the extra gelatin, and surround mold with chopped gelatin. *Serves: 10*

BOEUF STROGANOFF

Beef Stroganoff

You'll Need:

4 tablespoons (½ stick) butter
1½ pounds fillet of beef cut
 into small strips about 2
 inches by ½ inch (ask meat
 dealer to cut against the
 grain)
3 tablespoons frozen chopped
 onions

1 (6-ounce) can sliced broiled-
 in-butter mushrooms
½ cup canned beef gravy
1 cup beef broth
1 cup sour cream
 Salt
 Pepper

How To:

Put half the butter in a flame-proof casserole or frying pan.
Heat till foaming. Brown meat quickly and remove to a
plate. Add rest of butter to pan. Cook onions till yellow.
Add mushrooms, gravy, broth. Bring to a boil. Lower heat
and add sour cream slowly, stirring all the time. (If you
have a small wire whisk, now's the time to use it.) Return
meat to the mixture. Taste for salt and pepper, adding both
if needed. Serve at once. *Serves: 4*

Extra Touches: Sprinkle with chopped parsley or fresh dill.
If you like minute rice, you can cook it quickly while the
Stroganoff cooks, and serve the meat mixture on hot rice
or noodles.

POT AU FEU

Beef and Chicken in the Pot

You'll Need:

4 tablespoons (½ stick) butter
1 pound lean beef, cut up
  for stewing
5 chicken drumsticks or
  thighs
1 (13¾-ounce) can chicken
  broth
1 (13¾-ounce) can beef

broth
1 (12-ounce) can small whole
  carrots
1 (12-ounce) can celery
  hearts
Chopped parsley
Beurre Manié
Salt

How To:

Season meat with salt. Melt butter in a soup kettle and brown the beef. Push beef to one side and brown the chicken. Turn down heat. Add chicken and beef broth. Cover and simmer for ½ hour. Remove chicken, but continue cooking the beef for an additional hour. Just before serving, put back chicken. Add drained carrots and celery and (if you want to thicken broth) stir in 1 tablespoon of beurre manié, boiling and stirring about 3 minutes. Sprinkle with parsley. *Serves: 4*

Extra Touches: Serve in individual casseroles or in big soup plates, with a thick slice of toasted French bread in each plate. Pass grated Parmesan cheese. The more traditional way is to make two courses out of this dish; omit the beurre manié; serve the hot soup first with toasted French bread and grated cheese. Serve the meat and vegetables as the second course.

Pot Note: Have an extra can of chicken broth or beef broth on hand. Add if you want a soupier dish.

TOURNEDOS HENRI IV

Beef Fillets with Artichokes

You'll Need:

1 cup Béarnaise sauce (the kind you buy in jars is fine)
6 fillets cut 1 inch thick
4 tablespoons (½ stick) butter
6 toast rounds

¼ cup Madeira
¼ cup beef broth
6 artichoke bottoms
2 mushrooms, sliced

How To:

Heat the Béarnaise sauce slowly in a glass or enamel double boiler and keep it warm over hot water. Sauté steak in hot butter on each side for 3 to 4 minutes or until desired doneness. Place toast rounds on warmed platter and fillets on top of toast. Pour fat out of pan. Add wine and broth, cook up quickly, stirring all the time with a wire whisk. Cook 2 or 3 minutes. Pour over steaks. Place an artichoke on top of each steak. Garnish with sliced mushrooms. Spoon warm Béarnaise sauce over artichokes. Serve remaining sauce separately. *Serves: 6*

BOEUF BOURGUIGNON

Beef Cooked in Burgundy Wine

You'll Need:

1½ pounds round steak cut
   into small cubes
Salt
Pepper
1 tablespoon vegetable oil
2 cups canned beef gravy

1 cup Burgundy
1 (3-ounce) can sliced
   mushrooms
1 (8-ounce) can small white
   onions
Parsley or chives, chopped

How To:

Season meat lightly with salt and pepper. Heat oil in flame-proof (metal base) casserole. Brown meat. Add gravy, wine, and juice from the can of mushrooms. Cover casserole. Simmer till meat is tender, 1½ hours or more. Add mushrooms and drained onions. Cover and cook a few minutes. Sprinkle with chopped parsley or chives and serve at once. *Serves: 4*

Variation:
Omit onions. Serve with braised carrots or celery.

ENTRECOTE AU ROQUEFORT

Steak with Roquefort Sauce

You'll Need:

2 ounces Roquefort cheese
2 ounces cream cheese
4 steaks

Salt
Pepper

How To:

Mix the cheeses together until smooth. You might need a little cream to bind them together more smoothly. Season steaks and broil them for 3 minutes on one side. Turn steaks over. Spread cheese mixture on the raw side of the steak. Broil for 4 minutes or to desired doneness. Serve at once. *Serves: 4*

ENTRECOTE MIRABEAU

Steak with Anchovies and Olives

You'll Need:

4 small steaks
8 pats of butter, with a dab of anchovy paste* on each

16 anchovies
1 small jar pitted green olives

How To:

Heat broiler. Put steaks on rack with a pat of anchovy butter on each. Broil 4 minutes, turn. Put another pat of butter on raw side. Continue broiling another 4 minutes, or until done as desired. Arrange on a warmed platter. Lay anchovy strips on top of each steak. Garnish with olives. *Serves: 4*

Extra Touches: Serve with cold tomato salad.

* Buy it — it comes in a tube. It's mashed anchovies.

TOURNEDOS BEARNAISE

Broiled Beef Fillets with Béarnaise Sauce

You'll Need:

4 slices fillet about 1 inch
  thick
1 (8-ounce) jar Béarnaise
1 tablespoon chopped fresh
  herbs (parsley, chives,

tarragon)
Salt
Pepper
4 pats butter

How To:

Broil steaks. Heat Béarnaise sauce in the upper part of a glass or enamel double boiler over water. Add herbs. When the steaks are done, transfer to a warmed platter. Salt and pepper them. Put a pat of butter on top of each steak. (As they stand for a minute the juice and butter will make a dark gravy.) Spoon a little Béarnaise on top of each steak. Serve. *Serves: 4*

Pot Note: Loin lamb chops are delicious prepared in any of the manners suggested for steak.

TOURNEDOS ROSSINI

Beef Fillets with Foie Gras

You'll Need:

1 (2-ounce) can truffles,
  sliced
½ cup brandy
1 (4½-ounce) can liver pâté

1 tablespoon brandy
2 tablespoons beurre manié
4 tablespoons (½ stick) butter
6 fillets cut 1 inch thick

How To:

The day before: Open a can of truffles (it should contain 2 or 3 truffles). Slice truffles. Put them with the truffle juice and the ½ cup brandy in a covered glass container and store in refrigerator; reserving 6 truffle slices.

The day of the dinner mix the liver pâtè with a tablespoon of brandy and spread on a plate. Put 6 slices of truffles into the pâté at regular intervals. Place plate in refrigerator to chill. Prepare the butter and flour mixture. At dinnertime: Sauté fillets in hot butter 3 to 4 minutes on each side. When done as desired, remove and place on a warmed serving platter. Empty frying pan of fat. Pour brandy-truffle mixture into the frying pan and heat. Add beurre manié, stirring well. Put slice of the chilled pâté with a truffle in the center, on top of each piece of steak. Pour hot sauce over all. *Serves: 6*

BIFTEK MAITRE D'HOTEL

Steak with Green Butter

You'll Need:

6 slices steak   4 tablespoons (½ stick) butter

6 tablespoons green butter

How To:

Sauté steaks quickly in hot butter; 3 minutes on each side will do for a fillet, longer if you like it better done. Remove to platter. Put a spoonful of hard green butter on each piece of steak. It will melt by itself, making a sauce. *Serves: 2 to 4*

LANGUE DE BOEUF AU MADERE

Beef Tongue with Madeira Sauce

You'll Need:

1 (1-pound 6-ounce)
canned beef tongue
1¼ cups canned beef gravy

½ cup Madeira (or port, if
you are out of Madeira)
Chopped parsley

How To:

If you have a fire-proof shallow casserole that will also pass muster at the table, use it. Otherwise, any pot will do. Combine the beef gravy and wine, let it cook slowly for 5 minutes, stirring continually. If it seems too thick, add the jelly from the tongue. While sauce heats, slice the tongue and arrange it in the sauce, or arrange the slices on a warmed serving platter and pour the sauce over it. Sprinkle dish with parsley and serve. *Serves: 6*

Pot Note: To make beautiful slices, trim and cut the beef tongue on the slant. Hold the tongue so that it looks like a half moon with the two points down. Slice slantwise, starting at the thinner end.

LANGUE DE BOEUF AU GRATIN

Fresh Beef Tongue au Gratin

You'll Need:

1 (1-pound 6-ounce) boiled, canned beef tongue
½ pound boiled ham, sliced*
½ cup white wine
¾ cup canned mushroom gravy
1 teaspoon tomato paste

1 (3-ounce can chopped broiled-in-butter mushrooms
1 tablespoon chopped parsley
½ cup bread crumbs
4 tablespoons (½ stick) butter

How To:

Slice tongue. Arrange alternating slices of tongue and ham around the edges of an oven-proof platter. Since there is more tongue than ham, pile extra tongue slices in the center. Put wine, mushroom gravy, tomato paste, and chopped mushrooms in a pan. Cook and stir for 2 or 3 minutes. If too thick, add jelly from tongue. Pour sauce over tongue and ham on platter. Sprinkle with parsley and bread crumbs. Dot generously with butter. Brown under moderate broiler heat not too close. *Serves: 6 or 8 depending on how you slice it.*

* As long as the meat dealer is slicing the boiled ham, he might as well open the canned tongue and slice it too.

JAMBON EN CROUTE

Ham Baked in a Pastry Crust

You'll Need:

8-pound canned ham
4 (10-ounce) packages pie-
   crust mix
1 teaspoon orange flower

water (optional)
1 egg white, unbeaten
½ cup Madeira

How To:

Make pie crust according to directions on package, adding the orange flower water. Roll out and cover sides and top of ham with pie crust. The pie crust should be quite thick, almost ¼ inch, particularly on the top. Place ham in a shallow baking pan. Brush crust with unbeaten egg white. Bake at 350° for 1 hour or longer, according to directions on can. Some require longer baking. Make 2 cutouts in crust through which you can pour Madeira 10 minutes before serving. *Serves: 16 to 20*

Extra Touches: Surround with frosted grapes just before serving.

Frosted Grapes: Dip small bunches of grapes into unbeaten egg white, then put egg-coated grapes into a paper bag containing granulated sugar and shake. Place grapes on rack to dry. Can be made 24 hours in advance. Do not need refrigeration.

CHOUCROUTE GARNIE

Sauerkraut with Sausages

You'll Need:

1 (1-pound) can sauerkraut
½ cup cubed ham
4 knockwurst
4 thick slices salami

1 (1-pound) can small white
potatoes
Pepper

How To:

Combine the ham and sauerkraut in an enamelware pot and cook slowly for about 45 minutes. Brown knockwurst and salami in a lightly greased frying pan. Add to sauerkraut kettle with potatoes and cook till knockwurst is done. Use no salt. Season with pepper, if necessary. Serve in soup plates with plenty of bread and a jar of mustard. *Serves: 4*

Extra Touches: Any kind of sausage you can name can be substituted for salami and used in this one-dish meal. Small frozen potatoes can be substituted for the canned potatoes.

DUCK AND CHICKEN

CANETON AUX OLIVES

CANETON A L'ORANGE

CANETON MONTMORENCY

GALANTINE DE CHAPON

POULET SAUTE A LA MARENGO

COQ AU VIN

SUPREMES DE VOLAILLE SAUTEES AU CITRON

SUPREMES DE VOLAILLE A LA MILANAISE

PILAF DE FOIES DE VOLAILLE

POULET A L'ESTRAGON

CREPES DE VOLAILLE

SUPREMES DE VOLAILLE A LA PERIGOURDINE

POULET EN GELEE

COTELETTES A LA KIEV

POULET CHAUD-FROID

Duck and Chicken

When you say *Paris* . . . I say *duck*. It's an instant re-action. Duck with black cherries, pressed duck, duck with olives . . . For I remember walking the streets, map in hand, searching for the restaurants famous for duck.

After I had eaten all the duck in town, I went off in search of chicken. Coq au Vin is as French as a Southern Fried Springer is American. And I still remember, with fresh surprise, biting into a rolled chicken breast, crisp on the outside, tender and juicy on the inside . . . and finding no bones.

Some of these delicious dishes take to short cuts the way a duck takes to orange sauce. Some, sadly, don't. You'll find the takers on the next few pages. *Bon Appétit.*

Duckling with Olives

You'll Need:

1 (4- to 6-pound) duckling, cleaned ready to cook
Salt
Clove garlic peeled, or garlic salt
⅔ cup canned beef gravy
¾ cup canned chicken broth

1 (3-ounce) can sliced broiled-in-butter mushrooms
1 (8-ounce) can small white onions, drained
1 small jar pitted green olives, drained

How To:

Rub the duck with salt, inside and out. Rub with a cut garlic bud, or sprinkle lightly with garlic salt. Roast breast side up in uncovered pan in 350° oven, 25 to 30 minutes to the pound. Turn duck breast side down 30 minutes before end of roasting time. It is not necessary to baste since the duckling is usually fat. A fat duck takes care of itself. Remove duck to warmed serving platter. Pour fat out of roasting pan. There will be a dark gravy, not too much, in the bottom of the pan. Add all the rest of the ingredients and bring to a quick boil on top of the stove, stirring all the time. If the sauce seems a bit thin, add more beef gravy. Pour over duck. Serve at once. *Serves: 4 to 6*

Extra Touches: Sauté the duck liver a few minutes in 1 tablespoon butter. Slice and add to gravy. Pile hot browned potatoes (frozen) at each end of the platter, some watercress, and 4 baked half-tomatoes (2 at each end).

CANETON A L'ORANGE

Duckling with Orange Sauce

You'll Need:

1 (4- to 6-pound) duckling
cleaned ready to cook
Salt
1 clove garlic, peeled
1 orange, peeled, cut in 4
sections
⅔ cup canned beef gravy
1 cup red wine

2 tablespoons red currant
jelly
2 tablespoons grated orange
peel
2 tablespoons Cointreau
1 (11-ounce) can mandarin
orange sections, drained

How To:

Salt duck inside and out. Rub with cut garlic. Stuff with fresh orange. Roast duck breast side up uncovered in 350° oven, giving the duck 25 to 30 minutes per pound. If duck is fat, no basting is necessary. Or you may baste with orange juice 2 or 3 times during cooking period. When done, remove duck to a warmed platter. Pour fat out of roasting pan. Have all the rest of the ingredients measured out and ready. Put roasting pan on top burner, and add everything but the mandarin oranges. Bring to a boil, stirring all the time. Cook a few minutes. Add oranges and continue cooking sauce until oranges just heat. Pour sauce over duck and serve. *Serves: 4 or 5*

CANETON MONTMORENCY

Duckling with Brandied Black Cherries

You'll Need:

1 (4- to 6-pound) duckling
cleaned ready to cook
Salt
1 clove garlic, peeled
1 cup canned beef gravy
1 cup red wine

1 tablespoon currant jelly
2 tablespoons grated orange
peel
2 tablespoons brandy
1 (No. 2) can pitted black
cherries, drained

How To:

Salt duck inside and out. Rub with cut garlic bud. Roast duck breast side up uncovered at 350°, giving it 25 to 30 minutes per pound. Turn breast side down 30 minutes before end of roasting time. Place roast duck on a warmed platter. Pour off fat from roasting pan. Have all the rest of the ingredients measured out and ready. Add all except cherries to roasting pan, and bring to a boil on top burner of stove, stirring all the time. Cook a few minutes. Add drained cherries. Barely heat them through. Pour over duck and serve at once. *Serves: 4 to 6*

Extra Touches: Substitute brandied peaches for the cherries and leave out brandy. Cut peaches in quarters or smaller. Shoestring potatoes (they come in a can) are good with this. Heat in oven while duck cooks.

GALANTINE DE CHAPON

Capon Stuffed with Capon

A galantine is one of the more complicated of French dishes. It is a boneless fowl, stuffed with liver pâté or ground raw chicken, rolled into a cylindrical shape that looks like a very fat rolling pin. It is roasted or boiled and can be served hot or cold. A party dish, definitely.

This capon galantine is every bit as impressive as its more difficult sisters. Instead of ground meat or pâté, the fowl is stuffed with another fowl. There is work involved, but you don't do it.

Your poultry dealer bones two capons, each weighing about 6 pounds. He does this by splitting the skin and flesh down the back and slowly cutting out the bones. The rest of the skin must remain unbroken. The wing tips are simply cut off, leaving just the tiny drumstick-like bone to remove. And on the bird that is used for stuffing the entire wing is chopped off. One bird is fitted into the other. Then they are rolled and tied with butcher's twine (or white string) in three places, like a rolled roast. If the boneless legs hang loose, they should be tied together underneath the capon. The breast side is completely round and smooth. When you serve the galantine, the breast side will be up. So far you have not lifted a finger. You come home from the market with a package of boneless rolled capon, weighing perhaps 10 pounds. (The boning costs extra!)

You'll Need:

1 boneless rolled roast of capon (see above)	1 truffle
Salt	Butter or salad oil
Pepper	1 cup brandy, Madeira, or port

How To:

Salt and pepper the roll of birds. Slice truffle thin. Slide small pieces of truffle under skin of top capon by making a tiny slit in the skin with a sharp knife and pushing each piece of truffle in so the breast of the capon will have 5 regularly spaced circles of truffle showing. Rub roll all over with softened butter or salad oil. Roast in uncovered pan in a 350° oven, 30 minutes to the pound. Baste frequently with the brandy or wine, whichever you have handy. Turn roast 30 minutes before end of the roasting period. Test for doneness; use sharp-pronged kitchen fork. When juices no longer run pink, roast is done. The pan juices make a wonderful sauce just as they are. Serve hot on your best (warmed) platter, and carve at the table with a sharp knife. *Serves: 10*

Extra Touches: Artichoke bottoms (canned) stuffed with peas, mushrooms, or mashed chestnuts (chestnut purée) would be the right vegetable to decorate the platter. If you would rather serve your galantine cold, omit truffle, cook, and cool. Cover with jellied mayonnaise and decorate with sliced black truffles and bits of pimiento. Serve on a bed of watercress or shredded green lettuce.

POULET SAUTE A LA MARENGO

Chicken Marengo

You'll Need:

1 (3-pound) frying chicken, cut up
Salt
Pepper
4 tablespoons (½ stick) butter
1 tablespoon tomato paste
¾ cup (canned) mushroom gravy

½ cup white wine
4 eggs
4 big pieces of cooked lobster meat, or cooked rock lobster, shell and all
½ cup garlic-flavored croutons
Parsley, freshly chopped

How To:

Melt butter in large frying pan. When butter is hot, brown seasoned chicken on one side, then on the other. Reduce heat and add tomato paste. Pour wine and gravy over chicken. This should make a thin sauce. Add more wine now if it seems thick. Cover and cook slowly until tender, 20 to 25 minutes. A young chicken will be done. Cook another 5 minutes if your chicken is an adolescent. Uncover last 10 minutes. When the chicken is nearly done, fry 4 eggs. To make them neat, trim with a round cooky cutter. Set aside. When chicken is done, add lobster and just heat through. Add croutons. Immediately turn out onto a warmed serving platter. Sprnikle with parsley. Top with 4 fried eggs. *Serves: 4 to 5*

Extra Touches: Pile reheated frozen fried potato puffs at both ends of the platter.

COQ AU VIN

Chicken in Wine

You'll Need:

1 (3-pound) frying chicken cut in pieces
4 tablespoons (½ stick) butter
1 clove garlic, peeled
⅓ cup brandy
2 cups red wine (Beaujolais is recommended, Burgundy is fine)
Pinch of herbs, such as bay-leaf and thyme, or chervil
1 or 2 tablespoons beurre manié
1 (8-ounce) can small white onions, drained
1 (3-ounce) can broiled-in-butter whole mushrooms, drained

How To:

Heat butter in skillet, with clove of cut garlic. Remove garlic. Put in chicken. Brown quickly. Pour brandy over chicken. When warm, ignite brandy with match (don't burn yourself). When the flame dies, lower heat under skillet and add red wine and herbs. Cover and cook for 20 to 25 minutes or until the chicken is done. Thicken gravy by stirring in the butter-flour mixture bit by bit. Add onions and mushrooms, and as soon as they are hot, transfer to warmed earthenware casserole. Serve at once. *Serves: 4 to 6*

Extra Touches: If you have a small individual earthenware casserole for every diner, that will hold just a piece of chicken, an onion or two, and mushrooms and sauce, it makes a wonderful way to serve coq au vin. The whole dinner menu might read: Coq au Vin. Green Salad. Cheese. Pilot Crackers. Pot de Crème au Chocolate.

SUPREMES DE VOLAILLE SAUTEES AU CITRON

Chicken Breasts in Lemon Cream Sauce

You'll Need:

3 chicken breasts, split, boned, skinned, and pounded
Salt
Pepper
¼ pound (1 stick) butter
2 tablespoons sherry or vermouth

2 teaspoons grated lemon peel (you'll find it on the grocer's spice shelf)
2 tablespoons lemon juice (bottled)
1 cup cream
6 thin pats of butter
Grated Parmesan cheese

How To:

Salt and pepper chicken breasts. Sauté for 5 to 8 minutes in hot butter, turning chicken once to cook all sides. Remove chicken to an oven-proof serving platter. Put wine or vermouth, lemon peel and juice into frying pan. Cook a minute, stirring all the time. Salt and pepper sauce. Add cream slowly. Stir. Pour sauce over chicken. Put a pat of butter on each piece of chicken. Sprinkle with grated Parmesan cheese. Put under moderate broiler heat to brown. Serve at once. *Serves: 4 to 6 (makes 6 pieces)*

Extra Touches: Serve with frozen French-cut green beans. Cook according to directions on package. Drain and add a tablespoon of butter, salt, pepper, parsley, and, since you have all that lemon juice in the house, ½ teaspoon of lemon juice.

Pot Note: It is nice, but not necessary, to cook chicken suprêmes in clarified butter. It is also nice to use clarified butter for Beurre de Noisette or Beurre Noir.

The advantage: if the butter is clarified, you don't get little brown specks in the sauce. Does it matter? It depends on your eyesight more than on your taste buds. In candlelight it will never show.

But there may be a time when you want to try it the hard way. Make your clarified butter in advance, and store in the refrigerator.

How To:

Melt butter. A foam appears on top. Take the foam off with a large flat spoon and throw it away. (Or, see below.) The rest of the butter looks clear, except for a sediment on the bottom. Pour clear butter into a cup. Save it. That's your clarified butter. Throw away the sediment in the bottom of the pan.

Economy Note: Or don't throw away the foam. Put it in the refrigerator and add it to things such as soup and vegetables where butter doesn't show; it just flavors.

SUPREMES DE VOLAILLE A LA MILANAISE

Chicken Breasts Prepared in the Milanese Manner

You'll Need:

2 brown paper bags	Pepper
1 cup sifted flour	2 whole chicken breasts,
½ cup grated Parmesan cheese	split, skinned, boned, and
½ cup bread crumbs	pounded
1 egg	¼ pound (1 stick) butter
Salt	4 slices lemon

How To:

Put a cup of flour in one bag, and the cheese and bread crumbs in another. Break the egg in a soup plate, add about ¼ teaspoon salt and beat it lightly with a fork. Salt and pepper the chicken. Put all four pieces of chicken in the flour bag, close tightly, and shake it to coat the chicken with flour. Now dip the chicken into the egg and put into the cheese-bread-crumb bag and shake until they are coated with this mixture. Heat butter in pan till foaming. Sauté checken for 6 to 8 minutes or longer, turning them so that both sides are nicely browned. Decorate each chicken breast with a slice of lemon. *Serves: 2 to 4*

Extra Touches: Sprinkle half of the lemon slice with chopped parsley and the other half with paprika. Pour Brown Butter Sauce (Beurre Noir) over the sautéed chicken breasts, and then garnish with the lemon slice.

PILAF DE FOIES DE VOLAILLE

Rice with Chicken Livers

You'll Need:

1 pound chicken livers
7 tablespoons butter
2 tablespoons frozen chopped
  onions
1⅓ cups minute rice
1⅓ cups canned chicken
  broth

2 tablespoons grated Parmesan cheese
1 seeded, chopped fresh
  tomato
Salt
Pepper

How To:

Chop chicken livers into small pieces. Dry on paper towel. Sauté in 3 tablespoons butter over very high heat. Cook 3 or 4 minutes. They will be brown on the outside and juicy on the inside. Remove from pan at once, and season with salt and pepper.

Sauté onions in 3 tablespoons butter till golden yellow, but not brown. Add rice. Stir rice with fork. Heat chicken broth to a boil and add to rice. Add fresh tomato to the rice. Taste, and add salt and pepper if needed. Cover and let stand for 5 minutes. Make a bed of the hot rice. Place chicken livers in the center of the rice. Before serving, dot with remaining butter, sprinkle with Parmesan cheese. Put under broiler for a moment to melt cheese. *Serves: 4 to 5*

POULET A L'ESTRAGON

Chicken Breasts in Tarragon Sauce

You'll Need:

3 boned and skinned chicken breasts, split in half
1 or 2 (13¾-ounce) cans chicken broth
1 sprig fresh tarragon
1 (8-ounce) can minced

chicken pâté
1¼ cups canned chicken gravy
1 tablespoon chopped fresh tarragon

How To:

Cover the chicken with chicken broth to which you have added a sprig of tarragon. Cook slowly until meat is tender and done. Remove chicken. Cut a pocket in each piece. Stuff with a tablespoon of chicken pâté. Heat chicken gravy. Add the chopped tarragon and the stuffed chicken pieces and heat only until chicken is thoroughly hot. Serve at once. *Serves: 6*

Pot Note: How to find tarragon? Ask grocer and vegetable dealer or a kind friend with an herb garden. If no fresh tarragon is available substitute ⅓ tablespoon dried tarragon.

CREPES DE VOLAILLE

Pancakes Stuffed with Creamed Chicken

For Crêpes:

You'll Need:

½ cup pancake mix
½ cup light cream
1 whole egg

1 egg yolk
3 tablespoons melted butter

How To:

Follow mixing directions on package using the ingredients listed above. Heat a 12-inch pan. Grease it lightly. Pour a third of a cup of the pancake mixture into the pan and tilt pan quickly so that the entire surface is covered. The pancake will be very thin. Turn it carefully so as not to break. Make 4 such crêpes and stack them on a warm dinner plate. Keep them warm.

For Chicken:

You'll Need:

1 (12-ounce) can chicken à la king
1 (8-ounce) can artichoke hearts, diced
⅓ (5-ounce) can blanched almonds
1 (3-ounce) can sliced,

broiled-in-butter mushrooms, drained
¼ cup light cream
1 egg yolk
Grated Parmesan cheese
2 tablespoons butter

How To:

Combine and heat the first five ingredients. Beat egg yolk and cream, and slowly add to chicken mixture.

To Serve: Place one crêpe in bottom of a shallow buttered casserole. Spoon the solider parts of chicken mixture into center of the crêpe. Fold two sides of crêpe over chicken. Repeat with the three remaining pancakes. Casserole will be full. You will have used most of the chicken mixture, but some of the sauce will remain in the saucepan. Pour over crêpes. Dot with butter. Sprinkle with Parmesan cheese. Place under heated broiler to glaze top. *Serves: 4*

SUPREMES DE VOLAILLE A LA PERIGOURDINE

Supreme of Chicken with Truffle Sauce

You'll Need:

1 cup sifted flour	Salt
Brown paper bag	Pepper
2 whole chicken breasts,	¼ pound (1 stick) butter
split, boned, skinned, and	¼ cup Madeira
pounded	

Sauce

½ cup beef bouillon	½ teaspoon onion juice
1 chopped truffle, and the	(optional)
juice from the truffle can	

How To:

Put the flour into the brown paper bag. Salt and pepper chicken. Drop the chicken into the bag. Close bag tightly and shake till all pieces are coated lightly with flour. Melt the butter in a frying pan. When it foams, add chicken. Sauté for 6 to 8 minutes or until done, turning it once to brown evenly. Put chicken on a warm platter. Don't wash your frying pan. You are going to make the sauce in it.

Have all the sauce ingredients ready in a measuring cup before you start preparing the chicken. The liquid plus the truffle should just make one cup. Add everything at once to the frying pan in which you cooked the chicken. Stir over high heat for 2 or 3 minutes so that you get all the good bits that cling to the bottom of the pan, into your sauce. Pour over the chicken and serve at once. *Serves: 2 to 4*

Extra Touches: To turn this dish into an entire meal, you might add potatoes and peas. Start 5 minutes earlier. Put the contents of a package of frozen rissolé potatoes in the oven to heat. Open a can of French peas (they're the tiny flavorful peas). Put them in a pot and begin to cook them when you turn the heat on under the chicken. Cook the chicken as described above, transfer to the warm platter. Make the sauce. Let it wait in the pan. Pile oven-hot potatoes on one end of the platter. Pile drained hot peas on the other end of the platter. Now pour sauce over all. Serve at once.

POULET EN GELEE

Cold Chicken in Sherry Aspic

You'll Need:

4 boned and skinned chicken breasts, split in half
1 or 2 (13¾-ounce) cans chicken broth
1 envelope (or tablespoon)

unflavored gelatin
¼ cup sherry
1 lemon
1 small (2-ounce) can white truffles

How To:

Cover chicken breasts with the canned chicken broth. Cook slowly until meat is tender and done. Cool in the broth. Prepare gelatin according to directions on the package. Substitute ½ cup of chicken broth, the sherry, and a good squeeze of lemon for the required cups of water. Cool till slightly thickened. Coat each cooked chicken breast with gelatin. Chill in refrigerator until coating is set. Decorate each piece of chicken with a slice of white truffle. *Serves: 4 to 8*

Extra Touches: Use a slice of black olive as decoration on each piece of chicken. Chop left-over gelatin. Use it as a bed on which to serve chicken.

COTELETTES A LA KIEV

Chicken Cutlets Kiev

You'll Need:

2 chicken breasts, split, boned, skinned, and pounded	8 wooden picks (not the colored ones)
Salt	1 cup flour
Pepper	1 egg, beaten lightly
4 tablespoons green butter	1 cup bread crumbs
	1 cup vegetable oil

How To:

Salt and pepper chicken breasts. Put a tablespoon of cold green butter on each one. Fold over the two short ends. Then fold over the two long ends. Hold together with wooden picks. (It looks like an egg roll.) Dip in flour, in egg, and then in bread crumbs. Deep fry in hot oil (375° to 385° on frying thermometer) for 5 minutes or until golden brown on all sides. Drain. Remove picks. Serve hot. *Serves:* You'll have 4 cutlets. Most people take 1, but some people *like* chicken.

Extra Touches: Lots of watercress goes well with this. Carottes à la Poulette tastes good with this. If you are feeding a meat-and-potatoes man, serve a baked potato topped with a tablespoon of sour cream and a teaspoon of caviar.

POULET CHAUD-FROID

Cold Stuffed Chicken Breasts

You'll Need:

1 (2-ounce) can black truffles
  (soaked in brandy)
1 (7-ounce) can liver pâté
3 boned and skinned chicken
  breasts, split in half
1 (13¾-ounce) can chicken

broth
1 teaspoon lemon juice
1 envelope (or tablespoon)
  unflavored gelatin
1 cup mayonnaise

How To:

Chop one truffle and add to pâté. Cover chicken breasts with broth. Cook slowly until tender and done. Cool in the broth. Remove chicken and cut each piece in half horizontally. Spread with pâté and put the two halves of chicken together so that they form a rather high "chicken sandwich" filled with pâté. Repeat until you have used up all the chicken. Place chicken sandwiches on a wire rack. (Waxed paper under the rack will save some cleaning up later.) Take half a cup of chicken broth from cooking pot and add lemon juice. Empty envelope of gelatin into broth and heat until gelatin dissolves completely. Stir gradually into mayonnaise. Coat chicken sandwiches with this sauce. It will harden quickly. Before it becomes firm, decorate each piece with a slice of black truffle. Serve with garnish of lettuce. *Serves: 6*

VEGETABLES

HARICOTS VERTS, SAUCE BEARNAISE

CHAMPIGNONS AU SHERRY

BROCCOLI VINAIGRETTE

MARRONS

CELERIS BRAISES

LAITUES BRAISEES

RIZ VERT

CAROTTES A LA POULETTE

CONCOMBRES AU MENTHE

POMME DE TERRE AU CAVIAR

FONDS D'ARTICHAUTS, PUREE DE MARRONS

CHAMPIGNONS FROIDS

RIZ AUX TRUFFES BLANCHES

ARTICHAUTS MAITRE D'HOTEL

FONDS D'ARTICHAUTS AUX CHAMPIGNONS

EPINARDS A LA CREME

PETITS POIS A LA FRANCAISE

Vegetables

Vegetables are not an automatic addition to a main course. Dining in French, you might find nothing green on your meat or fish plate except a sprinkling of parsley. When the dish does have a vegetable, the meat and vegetable are so well mated, you feel that one was cooked for the other.

When a vegetable shines, it is a poor accompaniment. The shiners need a spot of their own on the menu. Perfect asparagus with a Hollandaise sauce deserves to be a separate course — perhaps the first course. A large, beautiful artichoke can certainly stand alone.

How to tell a vegetable that is a course-maker? Look at it. If it is large and beautiful and *looks* as though it will vie for attention, serve it separately.

Taste it. If the sauce *tastes* powerful enough to fight with the meat, keep the peace. Serve the saucy vegetable separately.

Green Beans with Béarnaise Sauce

You'll Need:

1 (9-ounce) package frozen whole green beans

1 small jar Béarnaise sauce

2 tablespoons sweet butter

1 tablespoon chopped green herbs (parsley and chives)

How To:

Cook and drain beans as described on package. Heat Béarnaise in upper part of glass or enamelware casserole over hot water; stirring in the butter bit by bit, and then the herbs. Pour over beans and serve. *Serves: 6*

CHAMPIGNONS AU SHERRY

Mushrooms with Sherry

You'll Need:

1 pound fresh young mushrooms, unpeeled

3 tablespoons butter

3 ounces (⅜ cup) sherry

How To:

Slice mushrooms. Sauté in butter for 3 minutes. Pour sherry over mushrooms. Stir, and cook 2 minute more. Serve. *Serves: 4*

BROCCOLI VINAIGRETTE

Broccoli Vinaigrette

You'll Need:

2 (10-ounce) packages frozen broccoli
Bottled Italian salad dressing

1 hard-cooked egg, chopped
1 (2-ounce) jar pimiento, chopped
8 black olives, chopped

How To:

Cook broccoli as described on package. Let cool. Under-cook if you are in any doubt. Drain and chill. Just before serving moisten with Italian-style salad dressing, and garnish with chopped egg, pimiento, and olives mixed together. *Serves: 6*

Extra Touches: Asparagus in the can, green or white, would save time here. Drain. Chill. And change the title of the dish.

MARRONS

Savory Chestnuts

You'll Need:

2 (11-ounce) cans unsweet-
ened imported chestnuts
Boiling water
1 cup canned chicken broth
2 tablespoons beurre manié

1 teaspoon tomato paste
1 bay leaf, crumbled
1 teaspoon Bovril
1 twist of the pepper mill
2 tablespoons sherry

How To:

Combine all ingredients except chestnuts in a sauce pan. Stir and heat until well blended. Drain, and add chestnuts. Cover and cook gently for 5 minutes or a bit longer. *Serves:* 6

Extra Touches: Add a 10-ounce package of cooked frozen baby Brussels sprouts at the end, and heat through. If the sauce needs thinning, add a bit more chicken broth. *Serves: 8*

Braised Celery

You'll Need:

1 cup canned condensed beef bouillon
1 teaspoon Bovril
1 small carrot, finely diced

2 tablespoons beurre manié
2 (12-ounce) cans stewed celery hearts
Chopped parsley

How To:

Combine first 4 ingredients in saucepan and cook uncovered 5 minutes, stirring slowly. It should have the consistency of light cream. Drain celery hearts. Arrange in an oven-proof platter or shallow casserole. Pour sauce over celery. Heat in moderate oven. Sprinkle with parsley. *Serves: 6*

Extra Touches: Add bits of crumbled cooked bacon along with the parsley.

Braised Lettuce

You'll Need:

4 heads Bibb lettuce
1 cup beef broth
1 small can cooked carrots (canned julienne-cut car-

rots would be perfect)
2 tablespoons butter
1 teaspoon chopped parsley

How To:

Wash lettuce thoroughly; discard damaged outside leaves. Cut each head in quarters. Arrange in bottom of large shallow casserole. Pour the beef broth over the lettuce. Arrange the carrots between the lettuce. Dot all with butter. Cover with aluminum foil, place in the oven at 350°. Let cook (braise) 20 minutes or a little longer. Sprinkle with parsley and serve. *Serves: 4*

Extra Touches: Hearts of romaine lettuce can be substituted for Bibb lettuce, but never use iceberg lettuce for this dish.

RIZ VERT

Green Rice

You'll Need:

1 cup rice, cooked
3 tablespoons butter
1 teaspoon dried sage

4 tablespoons chopped
cooked spinach

How To:

Stir butter, sage, and spinach into hot cooked rice. Serve at once. *Serves: 2*

CAROTTES A LA POULETTE

Carrots in Chicken Gravy

You'll Need:

1 (10½-ounce) can chicken
  gravy
3 tablespoons butter
⅛ teaspoon dry mustard
2 (14-ounce) cans whole

carrots
Sliced or chopped truffles
  for garnish
1 tablespoon chopped parsley
  or chives

How To:

Heat gravy, butter, and mustard. Drain carrots and add to sauce. Heat a few minute longer. Serve garnished with sliced or chopped truffles and chopped parsley or chives. *Serves: 6*

Extra Touches: The addition of 2 egg yolks can make a delicious difference. The preparation then is unlike that above: first, heat carrots in juice. Drain and place on warmed platter. Heat gravy, butter, mustard, and egg yolks, stirring constantly over low heat. Be careful not to bring the sauce to a boil or it will separate. Pour over the carrots and serve garnished as above.

CONCOMBRES AU MENTHE

Cucumbers with Mint

You'll Need:

4 medium-size cucumbers
¼ pound (1 stick) butter
½ teaspoon salt
¼ teaspoon pepper

1 tablespoon chopped fresh
mint or 1 teaspoon dried
mint

How To:

Pare and cube cucumbers. Melt butter in a pan. Add cucumbers, salt and pepper. Cover pan. Simmer gently for 10 minutes. Remove from heat. Add mint. Replace lid. Let stand for 2 or 3 minutes before serving. *Serves: 2 to 4*

Extra Touches: Pare 3 of the cucumbers and cube all 4. Looks better. Good vegetable with Quenelles de Brochet, Sole with Almonds, or Broiled Lamp Chops.

POMME DE TERRE AU CAVIAR

Baked Potato with Caviar

Large, perfect hot baked Idaho potato, with deep gash cut in it, topped with a tablespoon of sour cream and a heaping teaspoon of red or black pressed caviar. Good with Cotelettes à la Kiev.

FONDS D'ARTICHAUTS, PUREE DE MARRONS

Artichoke Bottoms Stuffed with Chestnut Purée

You'll Need:

1 (12-ounce) can puréed
  chestnuts
1 teaspoon salt
  Pepper
3 tablespoons butter

½ cup light cream or milk
1 can (6 to 8) artichoke
  bottoms
2 tablespoons green butter

How To:

Heat chestnut purée, treating it as you would dry mashed potatoes. Whip it with salt, pepper, butter and enough milk or cream to give it the texture of creamy mashed potatoes. Heat artichoke bottoms in green butter. Arrange on a warmed platter. Spoon chestnut purée into each artichoke bottom. Serve at once. *Serves: 6*

Extra Touches: Use a pastry tube to spiral chestnut mixture into each artichoke bottom. Good with roast or broiled fowl.

To Simplify: Heat canned large whole mushrooms in green butter. Place 1 mushroom stem side down on each artichoke bottom instead of chestnut purée.

CHAMPIGNONS FROIDS

Cold Mushrooms in Dill

You'll Need:

¾ pound fresh young
mushrooms
Lemon juice
Vegetable oil

Salt
Coarse-ground pepper
Fresh dill

How To:

Slice mushrooms very thin. Arrange in layers in a serving dish, quickly squeeze a little lemon juice over each layer of mushrooms to keep them white. You will probably use more lemon juice in this step than you need for flavor. Just before serving pour off extra lemon juice. Add enough oil to barely coat mushrooms, and salt and pepper to taste. Sprinkle with fresh dill. Serve very cold. *Serves: 6*

Extra Touches: If fresh dill is unavailable, put ½ teaspoon dried dill seeds in the oil and let stand for a few hours. Use chopped parsley for color. The mushrooms look well on a bed of watercress. Can be used as a salad or as a first course. Delicious as the main course of a summer lunch when served with hot French bread.

RIZ AUX TRUFFES BLANCHES

Rice with White Truffles

You'll Need:

2 tablespoons butter
2 tablespoons frozen
 chopped onion
1 cup rice
2½ cups canned chicken

broth
2 tablespoons butter
2 sliced canned white truffles
 Truffle juice from can
2 tablespoons grated cheese

How To:

Cook onion in butter till golden but not brown. Add rice to pan. Cook and stir 1 minute. Add broth and truffle juice. Cook uncovered till rice is done, about 25 minutes. If rice dries out, add more broth. Remove to warmed platter. Dot with butter. Sprinkle with truffles. Pass grated cheese. Good with chicken. Can be a main dish. *Serves: 2 or 3*

ARTICHAUTS MAITRE D'HOTEL

Artichoke Hearts in Lemon Butter

You'll Need:

1 (9-ounce) package frozen
 artichoke hearts
2 tablespoons butter

1 teaspoon chopped parsley
1 teaspoon chopped chives
1 teaspoon lemon juice

How To:

Cook artichoke hearts according to directions on package. Drain. Return to pan. Add rest of ingredients. Shake over fire a few minutes until butter melts and ingredients blend. Serve. *Serves: 3*

FONDS D'ARTICHAUTS AUX CHAMPIGNONS

Artichoke Bottoms with Creamed Mushrooms

You'll Need:

1 can (6 to 8) artichoke bottoms
1 pound mushrooms, sliced thin
Juice of ½ lemon
3 tablespoons butter
½ cup light cream
2 tablespoons grated Parmesan cheese

How To:

Sprinkle mushrooms with lemon juice. Heat butter. Sauté mushrooms for 2 or 3 minutes. Add cream. Stir and cook 3 minutes. Arrange artichoke bottoms in a shallow, ovenproof casserole. Pour mushroom mixture over artichoke bottoms in casserole. Sprinkle with grated cheese. Put under moderate broiler heat until cheese melts. *Serves: 6*

EPINARDS A LA CREME

Spinach in Sour Cream

You'll Need:

1 (10-ounce) package frozen   2 tablespoons sour cream
  chopped spinach   ½ teaspoon salt
1 teaspoon butter   ¼ teaspoon pepper

How To:

Cook spinach according to directions on package. Under-cook if you are in doubt. Drain well. Return to pan with teaspoon of butter, salt, and pepper. Heat. Take off stove. Add sour cream and serve. *Serves: 2 to 3*

Extra Touches: Use as a vegetable or as a bed for fried sole, sweetbreads, or veal; and as a creamed stuffing for crêpes.

PETITS POIS A LA FRANCAISE

Green Peas, French Style

You'll Need:

Bunch of scallions
2 (10-ounce) packages frozen small peas
Lettuce leaves
⅔ cup canned beef broth
¼ cup coarsely chopped ham
3 tablespoons butter
Black pepper, coarsely ground
Pinch parsley or chervil

How To:

Wash scallions, cut off and discard green tops, trim off roots. Combine all ingredients, except peas and lettuce, in a pot. Cook until scallions are tender. At the very last minute add frozen peas and lettuce and cook a few minutes till barely done. *Serves: 6*

Salads and Cheeses

What happens between the meat and the dessert depends on what you have eaten already. If you have eaten well, a salad will refresh the palate and allow you to savor the dessert. And if you have not eaten enough, this is the moment for a cheese course.

Salad

A salad that follows a meat or fish course should be light and clean and green. Some delicious greens are Bibb lettuce, Belgian endive, garden lettuce, and watercress.

Lettuce should not be sliced or quartered, or touched with a knife. The leaves should be separated with the fingers . . . and torn into manageable pieces with the fingers. Greens should be dry before dressing is added.

A French salad dressing like a French salad, is light and clean. It neither colors nor covers the greens. To make your own dressing, mix three parts of oil with one part of wine vinegar. Season with salt and pepper. Anything else is extra ...a pinch of dried mustard, a clove of garlic...

Don't toss the salad and the dressing together until you are ready to eat. Use only enough dressing barely to coat the leaves.

Cheese

Cheese, as a course, is served with French bread and butter, or, if you prefer, a bland cracker.

Cheese should be served at room temperature rather than at refrigerator temperature. Most French cheeses are eaten crust and all. Brie, Camembert, and La Grappe, unlikely as their crusts might look, are consumed in their entirety.

Serving cheese is a French custom. But once you have followed the French this far, you can be independent. You can serve an Italian or a Dutch cheese, a Canadian cheese, or a Wisconsin cheese, and still be very correct. Best of all, serve a Cheese Board, made up of a varied selection of different kinds of cheeses to suit different tastes.

Some of the easier to find French cheeses are:

Roquefort: A rather sharp, crumbly cheese, it is creamy white with blue-green veins.

Bleu: Looks like Roquefort. Tastes like Roquefort. But it is a bit softer in flavor, texture, and color.

Gruyère: Not strictly French, but from French Switzerland. You've seen the domestic version. Looks and tastes like Swiss cheese, except that it is often made with very small holes — or no holes at all.

Camembert: Ashy white on the outside and creamy yellow on the inside. Soft to the point of being runny. You might have to keep it at room temperature for several hours to achieve this state.

Brie: Tastes a little like a mild Camembert. Though the

surface is brown, the inside is that same creamy yellow. It is positively delicious.

Port Salut: Not as soft as Brie. A strong, full-bodied cheese, a Canadian version of which is called Oka.

La Grappe: A nice semi-hard cheese. Very showy, because the outside is covered with edible grape seeds.

DESSERTS

BRIOCHES AU CHOCOLAT

MERINGUE CHANTILLY AU CHOCOLAT

CROQUEMBOUCHE AU CARAMEL

CREPES SUZETTES JUBILE

BABAS AUX FRUITS

GATEAU CHOCOLAT AU RHUM

PETITS POTS DE CREME AU CHOCOLAT

PETITS POTS DE CREME A LA VANILLE

PETITS POTS DE CREME AU CAFE, SAUCE CARAMEL

BOMBE BOULE DE NEIGE

TARTE AUX FRAMBOISES

TARTE AUX ABRICOTS FLAMBEE

TARTE AUX POIRES

TARTE DE CREME AU CITRON

TARTE AUX FRUITS

TARTE AUX POMMES CHEZ MARIUS

TARTE AUX FRAISES

PECHES MELBA

PECHES AU CHAMPAGNE

PECHES AU VIN ROUGE

ANANAS AU COINTREAU

FRAISES AU SUCRE

FRAISES A L'ORANGE

GLACE A L'ORANGE

COUPE AU MARRONS

GELEE DE CAFE IRLANDAIS

GLACE AU CAFE, AMANDINE

GLACE AU CITRON

GLACE DE CERISES AU KIRSCH

Desserts

The dessert should end the meal with a flourish. If you have served a relatively simple meal, without heavy sauces or flaming swords, now is the time to come on strong with a great *Boule de Neige* or a French fruit tart made with your own two hands, or *Crêpes Suzette* (has anyone got a match to light the brandy?). But what is to follow a dinner that has already knocked their eyes out and sated their taste buds? After such a bang-up gastronomic experience, the understated, underacted dessert becomes memorable through sheer contrast. A lemon ice with a few crystallized violets, a fresh stewed peach served very cold, a tiny *pot de crème*.

BRIOCHES AU CHOCOLAT

Brioches with Chocolate Sauce

You'll Need:

4 brioches   1 small can or jar chocolate sauce

How To:

Warm brioches in the oven. While still warm, slice off the little knob on top. Pour 2 or 3 tablespoons chocolate sauce over each brioche. Put knob back. Serve while brioche is still warm. *Serves: 4*

Note: Brioche is a semi-sweet roll. This makes a very un-usual dessert. If sauce from can or jar is too thick, warm it slightly by placing the container in warm water. Stir and serve.

MERINGUE CHANTILLY AU CHOCOLAT

Meringue Cream Dessert

You'll Need:

1 package meringue mix
1 package éclair mix
Whipped cream

1 cup bought or homemade
chocolate sauce

How To:

The day before the dinner make meringues according to directions on the mix package. Bake in 10-inch flat round cookies on baking sheet, slow oven (275°) 4 minutes or as specified on mix package. You'll need 4 cookies. For the filling use filling from the package of éclair mix. (Or use packaged vanilla pudding as prepared in *Tarte aux Fraises*). Prepare according to directions on the package. Cool.

When ready to serve this dessert, combine the éclair filling with an equal amount of whipped cream. This makes a good pâtisserie cream. Spread some of this mixture on 1 meringue, cover with a second meringue and spread it with the cream mixture. Repeat using the 4 meringues to make a 4-layer cake. Pour chocolate sauce over the meringue cake and serve, cutting it with a knife warmed in hot water to keep meringues from crumbling. *Serves: 6*

Extra Touches: To the éclair mix add 2 ounces coarsely chopped semi-sweet chocolate, 2 ounces chopped candied cherries, and 2 ounces chopped dried citron, all previously soaked in a little kirsch. Decorate the top with more of the candied cherries.

Pot Note: If you can't find packaged meringue mix at your neighborhood grocer, the real thing is very easy to make. Below is a recipe which will produce meringues for Meringue Chantilly au Chocolat. They can be made one or even two days ahead of time.

You'll Need:

14 egg whites	2 teaspoons vanilla
¼ teaspoon salt	1½ cups sugar
3 cups sugar	

How To:

Use electric blender. Set at high speed. Beat egg whites and salt together till stiff. Continue beating, gradually adding the 3 cups of sugar, then vanilla. Fold in 1½ cups of sugar. Cover 2 cookie sheets with wet brown paper. Make 2 meringue pancakes on each cookie sheet. Bake in a 225° oven for 1 hour (or more). Turn off heat. Open oven door. Let the meringues cool in oven for 10 minutes. Then cool at room temperature. Peel off brown paper before using.

CROQUEMBOUCHE AU CARAMEL

Cream Puffs Iced with Caramel

You'll Need:

1 dozen small cream puffs
  (filled with custard and
  without icing)
1 tablespoon white corn
  syrup

1 cup lump sugar
½ cup water
Aluminum foil
Wooden picks

How To:

Buy cream puffs. Spread foil over your work surface. Set cream puffs on foil. Put syrup, sugar, and water in sauce pan. Cook over medium heat until sugar melts. Don't stir. Turn up heat until sugar is a light golden brown. Pour a little of this syrup over each cream puff. (Some will drip over onto the foil.) This is your caramel icing. While icing is still sticky, pile cream puffs on a round plate in layers to form a pyramid. Wooden picks will help keep the cream puffs in place. *Serves: 6* (2 to a customer)

Extra Touches: All of that caramel syrup that dripped onto the foil has hardened by now. Peel off from the foil and store hard caramel in a jar. Use it to decorate tarts, puddings. Or eat it like candy. It's delicious.

CREPES SUZETTES JUBILE

Thin Pancakes with Cherries

You'll Need:

2 packages (of 5) frozen cherry blintzes

4 tablespoons orange marmalade

4 tablespoons red currant

jelly

2 tablespoons water

2 tablespoons brandy

1 small can pitted black cherries, drained

How To:

Heat the blintzes according to the directions on the package. Combine the marmalade and jelly, add a very little hot water, stir to melt. Add brandy to taste. Add cherries. Heat and stir 1 or 2 minutes. Pour over blintzes. Serve hot. *Serves: 5*

Extra Touches: If small cans of cherries are not available, buy No. 2, and use 1 cup of the drained cherries. This makes a little more than 1½ cups sauce, or about 4 tablespoons on each serving of 2 blintzes.

BABAS AUX FRUITS

Rum-Soaked Cakes with Fresh Berries

You'll Need:

1 jar babas au rhum
2 tablespoons rum
1 pint strawberries or other

berries
¾ cup heavy cream, whipped

How To:

Heat babas, the sauce they are packed in, and the 2 table-spoons rum together until very warm, but not boiling. Re-move babas and arrange on a plate. Surround with fresh berries. Pour the warm sauce over all. Decorate with whipped cream and serve at once. *Serves: 4*

Extra Touches: Babas with Ice Cream: Warm babas and rum. Spoon 1 quart of ice cream onto a large chilled serv-ing dish. Arrange babas on top. Pour sauce over all. Eat the strawberries for breakfast.

GATEAU CHOCOLAT AU RHUM

Chocolate Cake with Rum Cream Sauce

You'll Need:

1 chocolate devil's food cake mix

1 (½-pint) jar rum sauce

1 cup heavy cream, whipped

½ cup chopped pistachio nuts

2 ounces sweet cooking chocolate, coarsely grated

How To:

Make cake from mix following directions on the package. Bake in a spring-form pan. This makes a high one-layer cake with a hole in the center. While cake is still warm, pour most of the rum sauce over it. Be gentle. Just moisten the surface. This will be the bottom of the cake. Turn it out to cool so that it sits in the syrup. Just before serving coat the top of the cake with the remaining rum sauce. Apply whipped cream to the top as you would a fluffy icing. Sprinkle with pistachio nuts and coarsely grated chocolate. *Serves: 8*

Extra Touches: Decorate with fresh strawberries that have been dipped in rum sauce. Fill center of cake with whipped cream. Top with strawberries.

Pot Note: To simplify, use frozen chocolate cake.

To make your own rum sauce, mix white rum with plain sugar syrup to taste.

PETITS POTS DE CREME AU CHOCOLAT

Individual Chocolate Puddings

You'll Need:

1 package chocolate pudding
2 cups half-and-half (milk
  and light cream)
1 egg yolk

1 ounce semi-sweet choco-
  late, grated
4 blanched almonds
2 tablespoons whipped cream

How To:

Prepare pudding according to directions on package, using
half-and-half instead of milk, and adding egg yolk. Add the
chocolate at the last minute. (The chocolate does not have
to melt.) Pour into little china "pots" or custard cups or
pretty little sherbet dishes. Decorate with whipped cream
and a blanched almond. *Serves: 4*

PETITS POTS DE CREME A LA VANILLE

Individual Vanilla Puddings

You'll Need:

1 package vanilla pudding
2 cups half-and-half (milk
  and light cream)

1 egg yolk
Crystallized violets
2 tablespoons whipped cream

How To:

Prepare pudding according to directions on package, using
half-and-half instead of milk, and adding egg yolk. Pour
into little china "pots" or custard cups or pretty little sherbet dishes. Decorate with a dab of whipped cream and crystallized violets. *Serves: 4*

Pot Note: You might have trouble finding crystallized violets. Try the deluxe import candy shops and fine grocery stores.

PETITS POTS DE CREME AU CAFE, SAUCE CARAMEL

Coffee Pudding with Caramel Sauce

You'll Need:

1 package vanilla pudding	coffee
1½ cups half-and-half (milk and light cream)	½ cup water
1 egg yolk	1 cup sugar
3 rounded teaspoons instant	1 tablespoon white corn syrup

How To:

Heat water, sugar, and corn syrup together in a skillet over low heat until sugar melts. Do not stir. Turn up heat. Cook until mixture is dark brown. This is the caramel sauce. Pour about 2 tablespoons of this hot sauce in each custard cup. Tilt cup so that sauce coats the entire inside of the cup. Make pudding according to directions on the package, substituting half-and-half for the 2 cups of milk called for on the package. Bring to a full boil. Turn heat down. Add egg yolk and coffee, stirring all the time. Pour into custard cups. Let chill and thicken in refrigerator. Turn out on cold dessert plates. Serve. *Serves: 4*

Extra Touches: Surround with salted almonds.

BOMBE BOULE DE NEIGE

Snow Ball

You'll Need:

3 pints vanilla ice cream
⅔ cup mixed candied fruits,
    chopped citron and red
    cherries are a good
combination
½ cup kirsch
1 cup heavy cream, whipped
2 dozen crystallized violets

How To:

Soak fruit in kirsch for 1 hour. Blend kirsch-fruit mixture thoroughly with the vanilla ice cream. Put into a 2-quart mold. Use pyramid or round mold, or a hemisphere-shaped aluminum mixing bowl. Place in freezer or freezing compartment of your refrigerator till ice cream hardens. You can make this part of the dish a day or even a week in advance, if you have a freezer. Unmold the ice cream onto a chilled round platter. Decorate with whipped cream. Arrange the violets decoratively in the whipped cream "snow."
Serves: 8 or 9

Extra Touches: Make a bed of leaves, using fresh violet leaves (from florist). Arrange little clusters of fresh violets around the base of the snow ball and a little cluster on top. Arrange a few more violets, decoratively, in the whipped cream.

TO MAKE FRENCH PASTRY FRUIT TARTS

Pie Crust

Make a pie crust ahead of time. Use a mix. Bake as described on package. Since a tart is an open-faced pie, one crust is all you need.

Waterproof the Crust

Before you fill the crust, waterproof it. This will keep the pastry from getting soggy. There are three methods: Cover the bottom of the pastry with very thin slices of sponge cake; or pour bread crumbs in the bottom of the pastry; or glaze the inside of the crust with the same glaze you use for fruit.

Cream Filling

A tart usually has a layer of cream filling underneath the fruit. This can be plain whipped cream or a mixture of whipped cream and vanilla pudding, flavored with liquor or almond extract. (It's called Crème Pâtisserie.)

Fruit

Beautiful fruits, canned, defrosted frozen, or fresh are drained and arranged on top of the cream filling.

Glaze

A thin coat of melted jelly (called glaze) is poured over the fruit. If the fruit is red, use currant jelly. If the fruit is yellow, green, or orange, use strained apricot preserves.

Pot Notes: You can prepare all the ingredients that go into a tart ahead of time. BUT. Don't combine them until the last minute. An hour is all that a tart can stand, if you want to present it at its beautiful, unsoggy best.

It is difficult to give exact measurements for a tart. In general a 10-inch pie crust will hold 1½ to 2 cups of cream filling and 2 to 4 cups of fruit to go on top of the cream filling. Or use more fruit depending on what kind you have. About ½ cup of jelly is needed for the glaze. *Serves: 6*

TARTE AUX FRAMBOISES

Fresh Raspberry Tart

You'll Need:

10-inch baked pastry crust
1½ cups sweetened whipped cream
1 cup currant jelly
   4 tablespoons hot water

Very thin slices sponge cake (enough to cover pie crust)
4 cups fresh raspberries

How To:

Make pie crust in the morning, using a mix. Just before serving, whip cream. Melt jelly with 4 tablespoons hot water; stir only until jelly is melted. Cover bottom of pie crust with thin slices of sponge cake. Arrange berries on top of whipped cream. Pour melted jelly over berries. *Serves: 6*

TARTE AUX ABRICOTS FLAMBEE

Apricot Tart, Flambé

You'll Need:

10-inch baked pastry crust
1 package vanilla pudding
  mix
2 cups half-and-half (milk
  and light cream)
2 tablespoons apricot brandy
  or plain brandy

½ cup bread crumbs
1 cup whipped cream
1 (No. 2) can apricot halves
  (drained)
¼ cup granulated sugar
¼ cup apricot brandy or plain
  brandy

How To:

Make a pie crust, using a mix, early in the day. Prepare vanilla pudding according to directions on the package substituting the half-and-half for 2 cups milk. Add 2 tablespoons brandy to the pudding. Cool.

To make the tart, get out all ingredients. Sprinkle bread crumbs into bottom of pie shell. Mix whipped cream and pudding together with a wire whisk and put mixture in pie shell on top of bread crumbs. Arrange apricots on top of pudding, skin side up. Work carefully. Sprinkle sugar over apricots. Put tart under moderate broiler heat for a few minutes until sugar browns. Pour warm brandy over the tart. Ignite brandy with a match. It will flame up quickly, so don't burn yourself. When the flame dies, serve the tart.
Serves: 6

TARTE AUX POIRES

Pear Tart

You'll Need:

1 package pie-crust mix
½ package éclair mix
1 cup whipped cream
1 (No. 2) can pear halves
1 cup apricot preserves,
strained
¼ cup water
2 tablespoons chopped almond praline

How To:

The day before the tart is to be served make an 8- or 9-inch pie crust out of a mix, and prepare half a package of filling from the box of éclair mix.

Just before dinner get out all ingredients and combine in this fashion: Add whipped cream to éclair filling, stirring well. (This make a pâtisserie cream.) Add bits of praline. Pile into baked pie shell. Arrange drained pear halves on top, rounded side up. Melt apricot preserves and ¼ cup water over heat. Let stand a few minutes, then pour a little over the pears. Sprinkle bits of praline around the edge.

(To make almond praline: combine 2 cups of soft sugar, ½ cup water, 1 tablespoon white corn syrup, and boil till brown. Add 2 tablespoons slivered blanched almonds. Pour out onto a sheet of oiled aluminum foil to cool and harden. Looks like a very clear version of peanut brittle.) *Serves: 6*

Extra touches: Add 2 tablespoons Cointreau to the éclair filling. If praline baffles you, plain almonds will do.

TARTE DE CREME AU CITRON

Open-Faced Lemon Tart

You'll Need:

8-inch baked pie crust
1 (3½-ounce) package
  lemon-flavored pudding
  and pie filling
⅓ cup sugar
¼ cup water

2 egg yolks
1¾ cups water
2 egg whites
¼ cup sugar
1 thinly sliced lemon
Powdered sugar

How To:

Using a pie-crust mix, prepare and bake an 8-inch pastry crust. Combine filling, sugar, and ¼ cup of water in a sauce pan. Add egg yolks. Stir with wire whisk. Add rest of water. Cook and stir over medium heat till pudding comes to a full boil and thickens. Remove from heat. Beat egg whites until foamy. Gradually add ¼ cup of sugar. Beat until peaks form. Fold warm lemon pudding into the egg-white mixture, working slowly. Pour lemon mixture into pie crust. Let cool but do not refrigerate. To serve, top with slices of fresh lemon. Dust all with powdered sugar and serve. *Serves: 4*

TARTE AUX FRUITS

Mixed-Fruit Tart

You'll Need:

10-inch baked pastry crust
1 package vanilla pudding
2 cups half-and-half (milk
and light cream)
2 tablespoons Cointreau
Enough thin slices sponge
cake to cover bottom of
pie crust

1 cup whipped cream
1 quart fruit
½ cup red currant jelly mixed
with 2 tablespoons water
½ cup strained apricot preserves mixed with 2 tablespoons water

How To:

Using a pie-crust mix, prepare and bake the 10-inch pastry shell.

Prepare vanilla pudding. Use a mix. Follow directions on package, substituting half milk and half cream for the milk. Add Cointreau. Cool.

Just before serving, heat currant jelly and water in one sauce pan till jelly melts. Heat apricot preserves in another till it melts.

Lay sponge cake in bottom of baked crust. Mix pudding with whipped cream, using a wire whisk. Pour this mixture on top of the sponge cake. Arrange fruits decoratively on top of pudding. Pour red jelly over red fruits and orange jelly over yellow, orange, or green fruits. Let stand only a few minutes, or serve at once. *Serves: 6*

Some good combinations:
Canned figs, defrosted sliced peaches, whole strawberries
Canned apricot halves and sliced bananas
Seedless green grapes, raspberries, and canned pear halves
Canned pineapple slices, canned plums, canned sliced peaches

Extra Touch: To make *Tarte aux Cerises Cognac* (Brandied Cherry Tart), substitute brandied cherries for the mixed fruit. Use only the red currant jelly. Mix 4 tablespoons juice the cherries were packed in, instead of water.

TARTE AUX POMMES CHEZ MARIUS

Apple Tart Chez Marius

You'll Need:

Open-faced apple pie or cake   ⅔ cup sugar

How To:

Buy an open-faced apple pie or apple cake. Dust the top with half the sugar. Put pie or cake under low broiler heat (2 or 3 inches from flame) till sugar browns. Cool for 5 minutes. Repeat, using remaining sugar. Serve warm.
Serves 6

TARTE AUX FRAISES

Strawberry Tart

You'll Need:

10-inch baked pastry crust
1 package vanilla pudding
2 cups half-and-half (milk
  and light cream)
2 tablespoons Cointreau

1 cup whipped cream
1 quart strawberries, washed
  and stems removed
1 cup red currant jelly
4 tablespoons hot water

How To:

Make pie crust in the morning, using a pie-crust mix. Make pudding, following directions on the package. Substitute half-and-half for 2 cups of milk. Add Cointreau. When you are ready to put the tart together, get out all the ingredients: pie crust, the pudding, the whipped cream, the strawberries, the jelly, and the water. Put jelly and water in sauce pan and heat till the jelly melts (about 3 minutes). Combine whipped cream and pudding, stirring lightly with a wire whisk. Pour this pudding-whipped cream mixture in pie crust. Arrange strawberries on top of pudding. Pour melted jelly on top of strawberries. *Serves: 6*

PECHES MELBA

Peaches with Raspberry Purée

You'll Need:

2 (10-ounce) packages frozen raspberries, thawed and drained

½ cup sugar

1 (15-ounce) can white peaches, drained, chilled

Fresh mint leaves

How To:

Put raspberries through a strainer. Combine strained raspberries with sugar. Put in electric blender for 3 minutes or in electric beater for 10 minutes. Chill. To serve: Pour raspberry sauce over peaches. Decorate with fresh mint leaves. *Serves: 6*

PECHES AU CHAMPAGNE

Peaches in Champagne

For each serving place one brandied peach and one large beautiful strawberry in a champagne glass. Fill with champagne. If fresh peaches are in season, substitute a peeled pitted whole fresh very ripe peach for the brandied peach.

PECHES AU VIN ROUGE

Peaches in Red Wine

You'll Need:

1 cup red wine	washed but not peeled
1 cup water	½ cup sugar
6 large perfect peaches,	1 tablespoon red currant jelly

How To:

Heat wine, water, sugar and jelly together in a glass or enamel sauce pan. Add peaches. Turn heat down. Simmer, uncovered, until peaches are nearly tender. Taste. You might like more sugar. Cook until peaches are tender. *Serves: 6, if the peaches are large*

ANANAS AU COINTREAU

Pineapple Cointreau

Select a fine ripe pineapple. Slice pineapple horizontally. (Do not cut off peel.) Re-stack slices so that it looks like a whole, uncut pineapple. Place a folded white napkin on a serving platter and put the pineapple on top of that. Serve. Pass powdered sugar and Cointreau. Make sure you have knives and forks at each place.

FRAISES AU SUCRE

Strawberries and Sugar

Select large sweet ripe strawberries. Do not remove stems and leaves. Put 2 tablespoons of raw sugar* in the center of each individual dessert dish. Surround with strawberries. The berries are eaten with fingers. Dip strawberry in sugar and bite off.

* Buy it in a health food store. It's brown, free-flowing granules. Maple sugar is also good.

FRAISES A L'ORANGE

Strawberries in Orange Juice

You'll Need:

1 pint strawberries

1 cup fresh or frozen orange juice

How To:

Wash and hull strawberries. Drain, place in a glass bowl. Pour orange juice over them. Set bowl in a bed of cracked ice. *Serves: 2*

GLACE A L'ORANGE

Orange Lena

Put orange ice in individual sherbet or champagne glasses. Top with mandarin orange sections and a tablespoon of Cointreau for each glass. Pass more Cointreau.

COUPE AUX MARRONS

Ice Cream with Chestnuts in Sweet Syrup

Top vanilla ice cream with a tablespoon of chopped chestnuts and the vanilla syrup the chestnuts are packed in. A dab of whipped cream on top of that.

GELEE DE CAFE IRLANDAIS

Jellied Irish Coffee

You'll Need:

1 envelope (1 tablespoon) unflavored gelatin
1½ cups hot water
¼ cup sugar
1½ tablespoons instant coffee
¼ cup Irish whiskey
2 tablespoons whipped cream
Dessert wafers

How To:

Put ½ cup cold water in sauce pan. Sprinkle with gelatin, let stand until gelatin softens. Add 1½ cups hot water. Stir and heat a few minutes until gelatin is dissolved. Add rest

of ingredients, stirring till blended. Pour into demitasse
cups. Place in refrigerator to jell. Just before serving, put
dab of whipped cream on each cup. Serve with dessert
wafers. *Serves: 6*

GLACE AU CAFE, AMANDINE

Coffee Ice Cream with Almonds

Toast and salt blanched silvered almonds, following directions on can. Serve sprinkled on top of coffee ice cream.

GLACE AU CITRON

Lemon Ice in Lemon Cups

Lemon cups are simply empty lemon shells. Cut a thin slice
off top, remove all the pulp. Fill lemon cups with lemon
ice. Put a crystallized violet on top of each. Surround lemon
cup with lemon leaves or any pretty green leaves.

GLACE DE CERISES AU KIRSCH

Cherry Ice with Kirsch Cherries

Surround each serving of cherry ice with a few drained
canned red pie cherries that you have soaked in kirsch for
½ hour. Use about ⅓ cup kirsch to the drained cherries
of a No. 2 can.

SAUCES

SAUCES BEARNAISE
SAUCES HOLLANDAISE
SAUCE REMOULADE
SAUCE BRUNE
SAUCE PERIGOURDINE
SAUCES MAYONNAISE
SAUCE MOUSSELINE
BEURRE MANIE
BEURRE VERT
BEURRE A LA MAITRE D'HOTEL
BEURRE DE CREVETTES
SAUCE DUXELLES
SAUCE POULETTE
SAUCE AU MADERE
SAUCE AU CURRY
SAUCE MORNAY
SAUCE DE TOMATE A LA PROVENCALE

Sauces

A sauce is not a blanket. You should always be able to taste the meat. And the fish. And the vegetable. The sauce makes them taste and look even better . . . that's all.

Some people love sauce. To them, it is the very essence of France, reduced in a pan. Others are on a diet. To please everyone, pour just a little sauce over the food and serve the rest of the sauce separately.

Warm Béarnaise #1

1 small jar Béarnaise sauce with a rounded teaspoon chopped fresh tarragon added. Heat in the upper part of a glass or enamelware double boiler over hot water, stirring all the time. Do not boil. Serve on vegetables, and as called for in recipes.

Warm Béarnaise #2

¼ cup white wine
¼ cup tarragon-flavored white
   wine vinegar
 2 peppercorns

1 teaspoon chopped frozen
  onion
1 bay leaf

Combine ingredients in glass or enamelware double boiler over hot water. Let boil slowly until reduced to 2 tablespoonfuls. Add to blender Hollandaise or to canned Hollandaise, with 1 teaspoon chopped fresh tarragon.

Cold Béarnaise

1 cup sour cream
1 tablespoon lemon juice
1 tablespoon fresh chives

¼ teaspoon salt
¼ teaspoon pepper

Combine all ingredients. Serve on hot or cold meats, fish, and poultry.

SAUCES HOLLANDAISE

Instant Hollandaise

To 1 small jar of Hollandaise, add a squeeze of lemon juice. Heat in a glass or enamelware double boiler over hot water, stirring all the time. Serve at once over hot cooked vegetables such as asparagus, broccoli, artichokes. And elsewhere as suggested in the recipes.

Blender Hollandaise

Put the following in blender: 3 egg yolks, 2 teaspoons lemon juice, ½ teaspoon salt, 1/16 teaspoon (pinch) cayenne pepper.

Start blender at low speed. Remove cover. Immediately add ¼ pound hot melted butter in a thin but steady stream. When all butter is in, sauce is finished. Makes ¾ cup. Serve with vegetables, meats, fish, as called for in recipes.

SAUCE REMOULADE

Rémoulade Sauce

One version: ¼ teaspoon anchovy paste added to half sandwich spread, half mayonnaise. Or, ¼ teaspoon anchovy paste, 1 tablespoon chopped pickles, ½ teaspoon chopped capers, and 1 teaspoon chopped fresh herbs added to 1 cup mayonnaise.

SAUCE BRUNE

Instant Brown Sauce

Canned beef gravy, thinned with red or white wine, half and half. Heat gravy until very hot but not boiling. Stir in wine. Serve as gravy with roasts, broiled meats, combinations of rice and meats.

SAUCE PERIGOURDINE

Brown Sauce with Truffles

Canned beef gravy, thinned with a little Madeira and truffle juice from canned truffles. Slice truffles and add with a little butter just before serving. Heat but do not boil. Serve with steaks, roasts, rolled roasts, roasts in pastry crust.

SAUCES MAYONNAISE

Blender Mayonnaise

4 egg yolks	¼ teaspoon dry mustard
½ teaspoon salt	½ teaspoon sugar
¹⁄₁₆ teaspoon (pinch)	2 tablespoons lemon juice
cayenne pepper	2 cups oil

Put egg yolks and dry ingredients and lemon juice in blender. Add ½ cup oil. Cover container and turn on low speed. Uncover immediately and gradually add the remaining oil in a thin steady stream. Turn off motor when the last of the oil has been added. Makes about 2 ¾ cups mayonnaise.

Curried Mayonnaise

1 cup mayonnaise with 1 to 2 teaspoons curry powder added. Beat well to blend. Use on cold cooked chicken, seafood, lamb, beef. Excellent for salads.

Garlic Mayonnaise

1 cup mayonnaise with 1 teaspoon garlic juice added. Beat well to blend.

Green Mayonnaise

1 cup mayonnaise, ½ cup mixed chopped fresh parsley, chives, dill. Blend cold mayonnaise and herbs. Serve as suggested with fish, etc.

Jellied Mayonnaise

2 envelopes (or tablespoons) unflavored gelatin heated in ½ cup light canned chicken broth or bouillon. When gelatin is dissolved, let cool until almost jelled, then add to 2 cups mayonnaise. A good masking sauce for chicken chaudfroid, cold salmon, etc.

Mustard Mayonnaise

1 cup mayonnaise to which 1 teaspoon of dry mustard has been added. Mix well to blend.

Sour Cream Mayonnaise

Mix sour cream and mayonnaise, half and half.

Tarragon Mayonnaise

1 cup mayonnaise plus 1 teaspoon tarragon vinegar, and 1 teaspoon crumbled fresh or dried tarragon. Beat vinegar and herb a little at a time into cold mayonnaise. Serve at once on meat, chicken, fish, salads, aspics, cold meats, and other roasts. Good on stuffed tomatoes.

SAUCE MOUSSELINE

Hollandaise with Whipped Cream

Mix 3 parts mayonnaise to 1 part whipped cream. Or mix cold Hollandaise and whipped cream in the same proportions. Delicious on cold chicken and turkey, with various seafoods in canapés, as garnish for galantines, aspics, and various gelatin dishes made of fish and vegetables.

BEURRE MANIE

Butter-Flour Thickener

Butter and flour mixed smoothly together, half and half. Good for thickening sauces. Have on hand. Add in small dabs to pan gravy in roaster or other cookery. Stir and let mixture boil about 3 minutes to cook flour.

BEURRE VERT

Green Butter

Using a fork, mix ½ cup soft sweet butter with 2 table-spoons of any kind of chopped green herbs and a few drops of lemon juice. Allow it to harden in refrigerator, and store until ready to use. Use on steaks, chops, and as noted in recipes. Freezes well.

BEURRE A LA MAITRE D'HOTEL

Lemon Butter

Add 1 teaspoon lemon juice, 1 teaspoon chopped green herbs for every tablespoon of sweet butter. Blend and add on top of hot fish, chicken, or meat.

BEURRE DE CREVETTES

Instant Shrimp Butter

Put ¼ pound (1 stick) melted butter, ½ cup cleaned cooked shrimps, 1 tablespoon tomato paste in a blender. Let it rip. Done in a minute. Refrigerate. Use as suggested in recipes. On canapés, fish in aspic, as cold garnish on hot fish platter.

SAUCE DUXELLES

Mushroom Sauce

Canned brown mushroom gravy, thinned with a little white wine. Heat and add a lump of green butter. Do not boil. Serve on meats, vegetables, meat baked in pastry crust, chicken, and roasts.

SAUCE POULETTE

Instant Chicken and White Wine Sauce

Canned chicken gravy with 1 tablespoon butter, one egg yolk, and a jigger (3 tablespoons) white wine. Heat gravy, stir wine in gradually, then egg yolk. Do not boil. Add butter just before serving. Serve hot with various chicken dishes.

SAUCE AU MADERE

Madeira Sauce

Canned beef gravy, thinned with a little Madeira. Add about 1 teaspoon butter to each can. Heat, but do not boil. Stir in wine. Serve with beef, veal, meat loaf, veal birds, etc.

SAUCE AU CURRY
Mild Curry Sauce

Canned condensed cream of chicken soup, thinned as described on can or with a little light cream and heated with 1 teaspoon of curry powder or more, according to taste. Stir well to blend. Do not boil. Use on cooked meats, fish, poultry, vegetables.

SAUCE MORNAY
Instant Mornay Sauce

Canned cheese soup, thinned with light cream. Heat stirring, do not boil. Pour over cooked broccoli, asparagus, other vegetables in combination with cooked chicken, turkey, or fish. Place under moderate broiler heat until top is lightly browned.

SAUCE DE TOMATE A LA PROVENCALE
Tomato Sauce with Garlic and Herbs

Tomato sauce, with a little chopped garlic, a sprinkling of fresh herbs (or equivalent), preferably parsley and chives. Optional, but nice, a pinch each of saffron and dried fennel, and a grating of orange peel. Heat but do not boil. Serve on meats, spaghetti, other pastas, barbecued meats.

A Word About Wine

Since using American ingredients and techniques to achieve *haute cuisine* is the theme of this book, I think it is appropriate in discussing wines to stick to the American product. They fit all the requirements of Instant Haute Cuisine — they are easily available, they are good, and an added plus, they are inexpensive. And I think there are few who would dispute the proposition that the good California wines are generally better, on the average, than the imported French, Italian, and German wines of comparable price.

Should you always serve wine with an *haute cuisine* dinner? My answer is yes. Wine at the table automatically and immediately proclaims an occasion. Even before it is tasted, a deep red or cool white wine in a handsome glass at your right hand gives the dinner an *élan* which no other drink can.

Must you serve a particular wine with a particular entrée? In theory, of course, certain wines "go" with certain types of food: dry white wines with fish, shellfish, and chicken; red with beef, cheese, and lamb. Rosé is traditionally served with chicken and turkey. In practice, within broad limits, you can serve whichever wines suit you best. A sweet dessert wine will not go well with tournedos, nor should a dry sherry be served after the soup course. But a dry white wine is very good with veal, and a Burgundy red is excellent with turkey.

The wide variety of brand names, generic, and type names which appear on the labels of American wine can be very confusing to the casual wine buyer. The generic names, almost all taken from wine-growing regions in Europe, give but a rough approximation of the taste of the wine inside the bottle. A more accurate measure to use in selecting a wine is the *varietal* name — the name of the grape from which the wine is made.

Below is a chart of wine grape varieties drawn up by Mr. Frank Schoonmaker, originally published in HOLIDAY Magazine, which lists the best of the California and Eastern grape varieties and their European equivalents. Since, obviously, the type of grape used to make the wine determines its taste, the varietal name on the label is your most important guide-post.

WINE-GRAPE VARIETIES*

CALIFORNIA	Varietal Name	Rating	European Equivalent
Red	Cabernet Sauvignon	The Best	Red Bordeaux
	Pinot Noir	Excellent	Red Burgundy
	Gamay-Beaujolais	Very Good	Beaujolais
	Barbera	Good	Italian Barbera
	Gamay	Fair	Beaujolais
	Grignolino (or rosé)	Fair	Italian Grignolino
Rosé	Grenache	Excellent	Tavel
White	Pinot Chardonnay	The Best	White Burgundy

	Varietal Name	Rating	European Equivalent
White	Johannis-berger Riesling	Excellent	Rhine
	Pinot Blanc	Very Good	White Burgundy
	White Pinot (really the Chenin or Pineau)	Very Good	Loire
	Traminer or Gewurtztra-miner	Very Good	Alsace
	Sauvignon Blanc	Very Good	Dry Graves
	Semillon	Good	Dry Graves
	Sylvaner	Good	Rhine or Alsace
	Gray Riesling	Fair	

EASTERN			Comment
All White	Delaware	Excellent	Also a good table grape.
	Elvira	Very Good	Special, pro-nounced bouquet.
	"Riesling"	Very Good	Not a true Ries-ling; much like the Elvira.
	Catawba	Good	Largely used in sparkling wine.

* Reprinted by special permission from Holiday, copyright 1958, by The Curtis Publishing Company.

Menus and Some Notes On Serving

Almost as important as the way Instant Haute Cuisine is cooked is the manner in which it is served. Remember, when you serve your dinner, that you have changed roles. You are no longer the cook. You are now the hostess. Actually, this is the hardest part of Instant Haute Cuisine: Switching your attention from the kitchen to the dining room. But the whole effect is lost if you can't perform the last chore.

You have prepared a meal that should require a staff of servants, and you have done it alone. You are not out of breath. Your intelligent use of short cuts has saved your strength. But has it saved your illusions? Do you think of yourself as the scullery maid, or as the lady of the house who is entertaining friends, this time at dinner?

At first you might not be too sure. So here are a few suggestions to take you over the transition period. Later you will make the leap, instantly, and alone.

Look at the food with a pleasant but detached smile. Never cast an anxious glance at a platter or at a person. Pretend the whole thing was catered. Don't talk about the food! If someone says how delicious the trout is, don't reply, "Really, it's frozen, and it took only four minutes to make." And if you hear a pleasant comment on the quiche, don't be chatty and go on about how much better it turned out the last time you made it.

Good food contributes to good conversation, but it doesn't make good conversation. Hard as it is to face this fact after you have personally worked on a dish, the food is only subliminally the star of the dinner party. The food, if it is good, flatters and pleases your guests so that they become their best and most entertaining selves . . . that's all.

If someone asks for a recipe, don't hesitate. Say yes. Offer to telephone in the morning . . . or to write it out and mail it the next day. And then change the subject. You are not giving away any secrets. After all, Escoffier published all of his recipes, and how many times have you eaten an "Escoffier dinner" when you've been invited out?

Don't wear an apron, even one of those frilly hostessy ones, when you are out of the kitchen. It creates the wrong image. If you spill something on yourself in the course of duty, *c'est la guerre.* Remember that your guests run the same danger bravely without an apron. A glass of red wine could spill over a white shirt with the jar of an elbow.

Don't ask your husband to help you do *anything.* In France the husband is the head of the house. If you are cooking in French, he will have to be the head of the house, during meals.

There is no section in this book on table settings, because the *décor* of the French table — in private homes and at the most chic of restaurants — is almost always simple, not to say severe. What you eat and drink is the center of attraction, and if anything is to be dressed up, it is the food, not the table. Traditionally a white table cloth is spread with plates, glasses, and silver, and perhaps a few flowers in a small vase. Against a plain background such as this, a Gigot d'Agneau en Croûte or even Petits Pots de Crème will contrast all the more spectacularly.

MENUS

Here are a few ideas for meals made up from Instant Haute Cuisine recipes. Those in the first group are designed for use as lunches or light suppers. Those in the second group are for full scale dinners. Even though the French don't always drink coffee at the end of the meal as we do, it is listed in each of the menus.

Lunch or Supper Menus

POTAGE PUREE DE POIS	Cold Curried Pea Soup
POULET CHAUD-FROID	Cold Stuffed Chicken Breasts
SALADE DE RIZ	Rice Salad
FRAISES À L'ORANGE	Strawberries in Orange Juice
CAFE	Coffee

FONDUE BOURGUIGNONNE	Beef Fondue
FRUITS	Fresh Fruit
LES FROMAGES	Cheese Board
CAFE	Coffee

CONSOMME BELLEVUE	Clam and Chicken Broth
QUICHE LORRAINE	Egg Custard, Ham and Cheese Tart
SALADE	Salad
GLACE AU CAFE, AMANDINE	Coffee Ice Cream with Almonds
CAFE	Coffee

PATE MAISON	Pâté Maison (with pistachio nuts instead of truffles)
BOUILLABAISSE	Fish Stew
SALADE	Salad
PECHES AU VIN ROUGE	Peaches in Red Wine
CAFE	Coffee

CONSOMME MELANGE	Chicken and Beef Broth
QUENELLES DE BROCHET	Fish Quenelles in Shrimp Sauce
CONCOMBRES AU MENTHE	Cucumbers with Mint
GLACE A L'ORANGE	Orange Ice and Cointreau
CAFE	Coffee

CORNETS DE JAMBON	Stuffed Ham Cones
CREVETTES AU CURRY	Curried Shrimp in a
RIZ	Ring of Rice
SALADE	Salad
GATEAU CHOCOLAT AU RHUM	Chocolate Cake with Rum Cream Sauce
CAFE	Coffee

SOUPE A L'OIGNON	Individual Casseroles of Onion Soup
ESCARGOTS A LA BOURGUIGNONNE	Little Platters of Snails
PORT-SALUT, ROQUEFORT, BRIE	Cheese Board
TARTE AUX FRAISES	Strawberry Tart
CAFE	Coffee

Dinner Menus

RADIS AU BEURRE	Radishes with Butter
BOULA BOULA	Green Pea and Turtle Soup with Sherry
GALANTINE DE CHAPON	Capon Stuffed with Capon
RIZ VERT	Green Rice
FOND D'ARTICHAUTS AUX CHAMPIGNONS	Artichoke Bottoms with Creamed Mushrooms
BABAS AUX FRUITS	Rum-Soaked Cakes with Fresh Berries
CAFE	Coffee

POTAGE CINGALAISE	Cold Curried Cream of Chicken Soup
JAMBON EN CROUTE	Ham baked in a Pastry Crust
PETITS POIS A LA FRANCAISE	Green Peas, French Style
CAROTTES A LA POULETTE	Carrots in Chicken Gravy
SALADE	Salad
BOMBE BOULE DE NEIGE	Snow Ball
CAFE	Coffee

ASPERGES HOLLANDAISE	Asparagus with Hollandaise Sauce
CANETON A L'ORANGE	Duckling with Orange Sauce
POMMES DE TERRE	Potato Puffs
SALADE ET FROMAGES	Salad and Cheese
COUPE AUX MARRONS	Ice Cream with Chestnuts
CAFE	Coffee

OEUFS EN GELEE	Eggs in Aspic
BOEUF BOURGUIGNON	Beef Cooked in Burgundy Wine
HARICOTS VERTS MAITRE D'HOTEL	French Cut Green Beans with Lemon Butter
LES FROMAGES	Cheese Board
PECHES MELBA	Peaches with Raspberry Sauce
CAFE	Coffee

ARTICHAUTS FROIDS	Cold Artichokes with Caviar
SUPREMES DE VOLAILLE SAUTEES AU CITRON	Chicken Breasts in Lemon Cream Sauce
POMMES DE TERRE RISSOLEES	Little Browned Potatoes
SALADE	Salad
MERINGUE CHANTILLY AU CHOCOLAT	Chocolate Meringue Cream Dessert
CAFE	Coffee

POTAGE CREME DE CRESSON	Cream of Watercress Soup
SUPREMES DE VOLAILLE A LA MILANAISE	Chicken Breasts Prepared in the Milanese Manner
CHAMPIGNONS AU SHERRY	Mushrooms with Sherry
LES FROMAGES	Cheese Board
TARTE AUX FRUITS	Mixed-Fruit Tart
CAFE	Coffee

SAUMON FUME	Smoked Salmon
TOURNEDOS HENRI IV	Beef Fillets with Artichokes
POMMES DE TERRE FRITES	Fried Potatoes
CELERIS BRAISES	Braised Celery
SALADE ET FROMAGES	Salad and Cheese
CROQUEMBOUCHE AU CARAMEL	Cream Puffs Iced with Caramel
CAFE	Coffee

BORSCHT	Beet Soup
BOEUF STROGANOFF	Beef Stroganoff in a
RIZ	Ring of Rice
PETITS POIS A LA FRANCAISE	Green Peas, French Style
LES FROMAGES	Cheese Board
ANANAS AU COINTREAU	Pineapple with Cointreau
CAFE	Coffee

PATE EN GELEE	Pâté in Ruby Jelly
LANGUOSTE A L'ARMORICAINE	Lobster in Tomato Sauce with Brandy
RIZ	Buttered Rice
ARTICHAUTS MAITRE D'HOTEL	Artichoke Hearts in Lemon Butter
SALADE	Salad
TARTE AUX POMMES CHEZ MARIUS	Open-Faced Apple Cake
CAFE	Coffee

SAUCISSONS	Platter of Sausages
TRUITE AU BLEU	Trout in Butter Sauce
POMMES DE TERRE	Boiled Potatoes
SALADE	Salad
PETIT POT DE CREME AU CAFE, SAUCE CARAMEL	Coffee Pudding with Caramel Sauce
CAFE	Coffee

Index